D0788875

Art in Context

Turner: Rain, Steam and Speed

Art in Context

Edited by John Fleming and Hugh Honour

Each volume in this series discusses a famous painting or sculpture as both image and idea in its context – whether stylistic, technical, literary, psychological, religious, social or political. In what circumstances was it conceived and created? What did the artist hope to achieve? What means did he employ, subconscious or conscious? Did he succeed? Or how far did he succeed? His preparatory drawings and sketches often allow us some insight into the creative process and other artists' renderings of the same or similar themes help us to understand his problems and ambitions. Technique and his handling of the medium are fascinating to watch close up. And the work's impact on contemporaries and its later influence on other artists can illuminate its meaning for us today.

By focusing on these outstanding paintings and sculptures our understanding of the artist and the world in which he lived is sharpened. But since all great works of art are unique and every one presents individual problems of understanding and appreciation, the authors of these volumes emphasize whichever aspects seem most relevant. And many great masterpieces, too often and too easily accepted and dismissed because they have become familiar, are shown to contain further and deeper layers of meaning for us.

Art in Context

***Joseph Mallord William Turner**, painter and engraver, was born in London on 23 April 1775 and died there on 19 December 1851. His father was a barber. He was trained in London and attended the Royal Academy Schools from 1789. He first exhibited in 1790, became an A.R.A. in 1799 and a R.A. in 1802. He held the office of Professor of Perspective at the Academy from 1807–37. He first went abroad, to France and Switzerland, in 1802, and made many subsequent visits to the Continent, especially to Venice and Switzerland. After 1800 his work was often severely criticized and ridiculed, but the publication of Ruskin's* Modern Painters *from 1843 broadened his reputation.*

***Rain, Steam and Speed: The Great Western Railway** is painted in oil on canvas (91 x 122 cm). It was painted in 1844 and exhibited the Royal Academy the same year. Turner bequeathed it, together with many other paintings, to Great Britain and it has been in the National Gallery, London, since 1865.*

The Viking Press, Inc.

Turner: Rain, Steam and Speed

John Gage

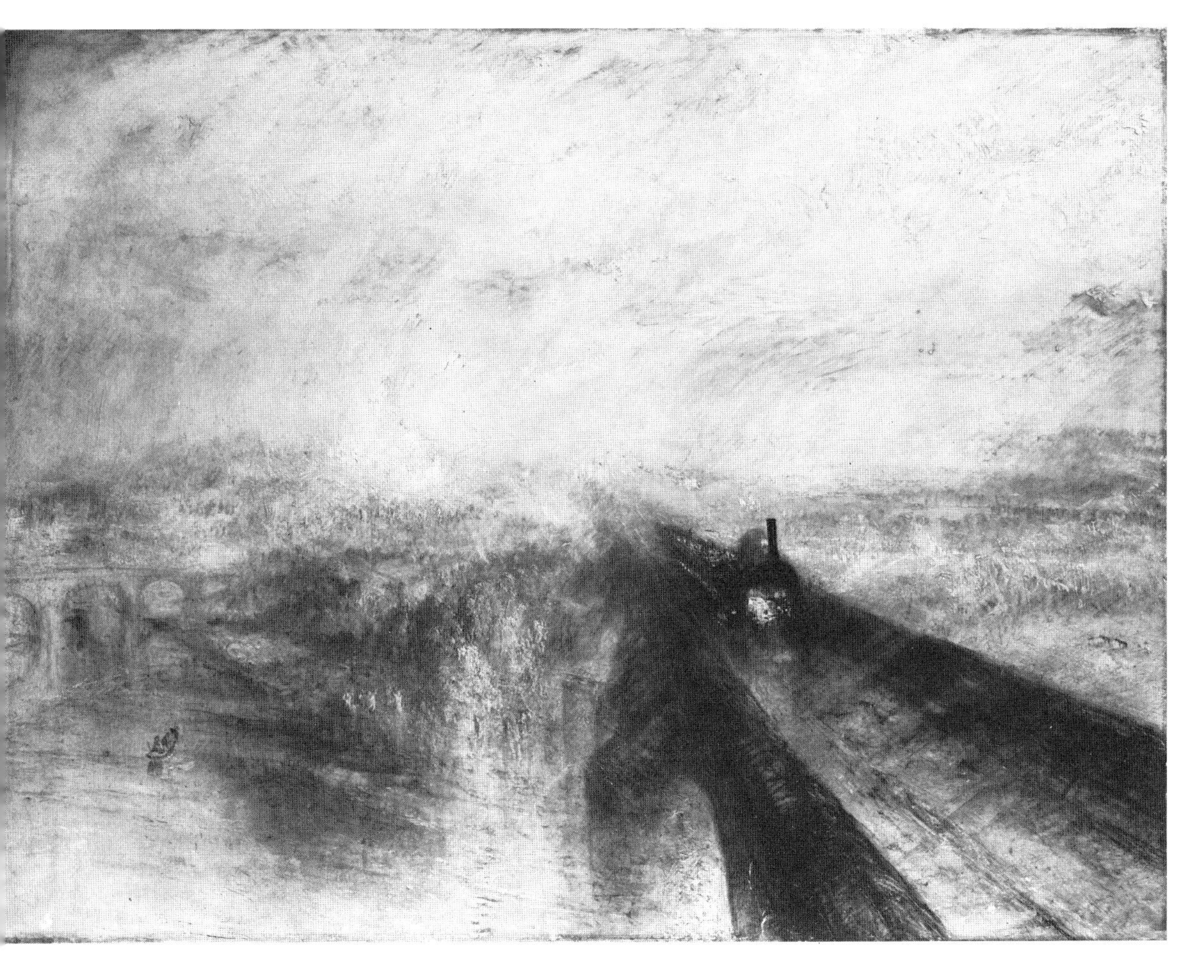

Published in 1972 by The Viking Press, Inc., 625 Madison Avenue, New York, N.Y. 10022
SBN 670-73289-3
Library of Congress catalog card number: 72-161061
Filmset in Monophoto Ehrhardt by Oliver Burridge Filmsetting Ltd, Crawley, England
Color plate printed photogravure by D. H. Greaves Ltd, Scarborough, England
Printed and bound by Jarrolds, Norwich, England

Designed by Gerald Cinamon

Reference colour plate at end of book

Historical Table

1825	First steam locomotive railway (Stockton–Darlington)
1826	
1828	
1829	Stephenson's *Rocket*
1830	Accession of William IV Revolution in Paris
1831	
1832	Reform Bill passed
1833	
1834	End of slavery in British Empire
1836	First train in London (to Greenwich)
1837	Accession of Queen Victoria First patent for Electric Telegraph
1838	People's Charter First steamship service England–U.S.A. Opening of Great Western Railway First state railway (Brunswick)
1839	
1840	Queen Victoria marries Albert Introduction of Penny Post
1841	First Bradshaw *Railway Guide*
1843	Opening of Brunel's Thames Tunnel
1844	
1845	
1846	Standardization of British railway gauge
1848	Revolutions in Europe
1850	
1851	Great Exhibition First submarine cable (Dover–Calais) *Coup d'état* of Louis Napoleon

Death of J. L. David		
Constable's Canal-scape *The Leaping Horse*		
John Martin's *Deluge*		1826
	Brougham founds Society for the Diffusion of Useful Knowledge	1827
Death of Goya		1828
John Martin's *Fall of Niniveh*		
Turner's *Ulysses deriding Polyphemus*		1829
	Cobbett's *Rural Rides*	1830
Delacroix's *Liberty Leading the People*	Darwin begins *Beagle* voyage	1831
Turner's first Venetian painting	Start of Oxford Movement	1833
	Birth of William Morris	1834
Death of Constable		1837
Turner's *The Fighting Temeraire*	Photography publicized	1839
Birth of Monet		1840
Turner's *The Slave Ship*		
	Ruskin's *Modern Painters I*	1843
Turner: *Rain, Steam and Speed*	Wordsworth's *Kendal and Windermere Railway*	1844
John Martin's *Plan of the London Connecting Railway*	Engels' *Situation of the Working Classes in England*	1845
	Dickens edits first cheap English newspaper *(Daily News)*	1846
	First parts of *Dombey and Son*	
Pre-Raphaelite Brotherhood formed	*Communist Manifesto*	1848
Millais's *Christ in the House of His Parents* attacked by Dickens	Death of Wordsworth	1850
Courbet's *Stonebreakers*	Publication of *The Prelude*	
Death of Turner		1851

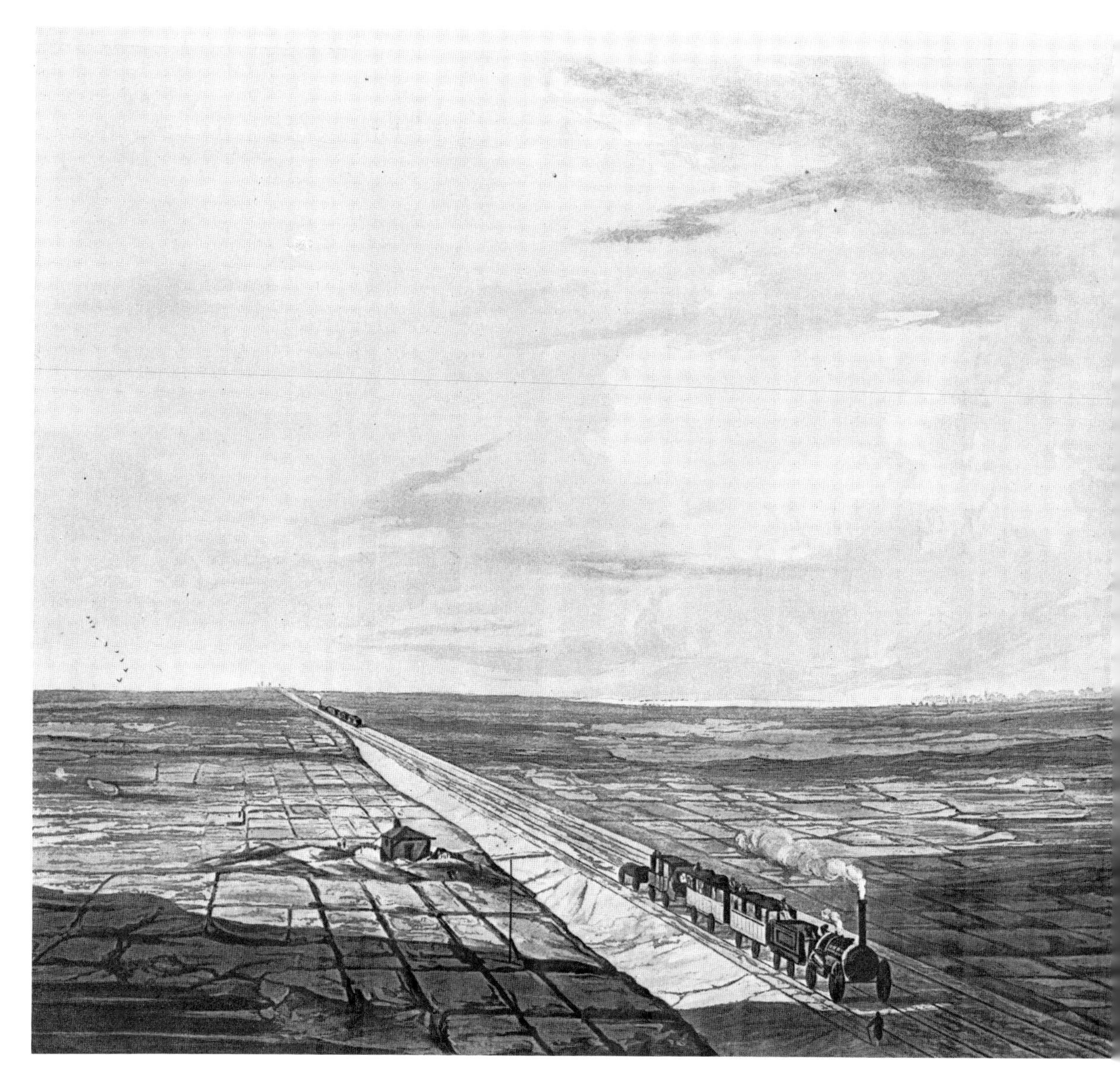

1. The Artist and the Railway Age

1. *The Railway over Chat Moss*, 1831. T. T. Bury

In the spring of 1844 the Railway Mania, which had been shaking England for nearly a decade, entered upon its final and most manic phase. During the year the unprecedented number of 220 Bills to sanction new lines was introduced into Parliament, and Gladstone took the step of bringing all new projects under government surveillance and control, even to the extent of proposing that the British railways might be purchased and consolidated by the State. Railway Shares had achieved the solid, if unexciting, status of Consols, and it seemed that the development was so momentous as to imply a species of Divine Intervention in human affairs:

'Edifying sermons proved that railways were prophesied by the seers of old, and Ezechiel was expounded to sanction and to sanctify the iron way. Leading articles dilated with energy and eloquence upon its prospects. "Nor indeed," wrote one, "can we contemplate unmoved the glorious prospect which will be opened to the world, if merely the vast and important works now in progress – works with which the useless Egyptian pyramids or the vaunted remnants of old Rome's extravagance, will not endure comparison, be carried into execution. The length of our lives, so far as regards the power of acquiring information and disseminating power, will be doubled, and we may be justified in looking for the arrival of a time when the whole world will have become one great family, speaking one language, governed in unity by like laws, and adoring one God".'[1]

In their effect, the railways were, above all things, the creators of modern Empire:

'Omnipresence is one of the principles of their progress. Not content with making Liverpool their lineage home, and many-sounding Manchester mistress of their choice, they are throwing

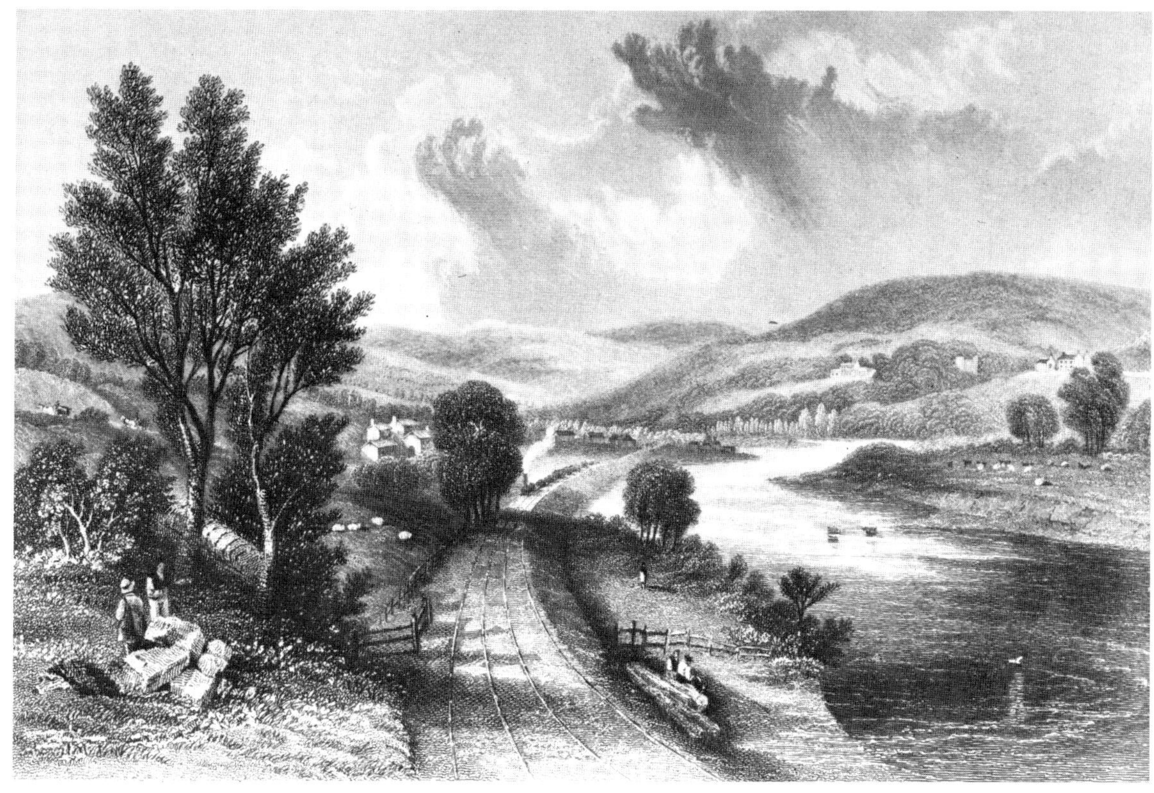

2. *Ridley Hall*, 1836. J. W. Carmichael

a girdle round the globe itself. Far-off India woos them over its waters and China listens to the voice of the charmer. The ruined hills and broken altars of Greece, will soon re-echo to the whistle of the locomotive, or be converted to shrines sacred to commerce, by the power of those magnificent agencies by which the rivers are spanned, territories traversed, commerce enfranchised, confederacies consolidated; by which the adamantine is made divisible, and man assumes a lordship over time and space.'[2]

This was the long view, but on a more local plane, it was clear to the British public that the most signal triumph of that spring would be the opening of the Bristol and Exeter extension of the Great Western Railway, completing nearly two hundred miles of line in the West of England. 'May', wrote *The Times*, with uncharacteristic reticence on 27 April 1844, 'thus has quite its share of interesting railway occurrences.' May, too, was the opening month of the Royal Academy Exhibition; but there was, on this occasion, as usual, a general indifference to these momentous events shown by the practitioners of Fine Arts, with the exception of the architects, whose exhibited drawings had, in the thirties and forties, documented the expanding rail network with designs of increasingly imperial grandeur. A number of railway guidebooks had already appeared, illustrated sometimes with engravings of exceptional quality [1, 2],[3] but among the more ambitious and the more imaginative painters there seems to have been no response; with the single exception of J. M. W. Turner, who at this Academy of 1844 showed his *Rain, Steam and Speed: The Great Western Railway*, now in the National Gallery in London.

Rain, Steam and Speed was certainly the odd-man-out among the three marine and three Venetian scenes which Turner exhibited that year; but it was neither a large nor a pretentious picture, and it seems to have attracted no more and no less praise or blame than was usual among Turner's critics of this period:

'Turner comes out this year with all his wonted peculiarities [wrote *The Times* on May 8] so that he will neither lose a determined admirer nor win one vote from those who are accustomed to attack his extraordinary productions. The "Approach to Venice" [now in the National Gallery of Art in Washington], with its rich greens in the foreground and the tints of the clouds and of the distant objects, all so delicately blended, presents a beautiful and fantastic display of colours to the spectator, who will take his station amid the benches in the middle room, and be content with the general impression. The railways have furnished Turner with a new field for the exhibition of his eccentric style. His "Rain, Steam, and Speed" shows the Great Western in a very sudden perspective, and the dark atmosphere, the bright sparkling fire of the engine, and the dusky smoke, form a very striking combination. Whether Turner's pictures are dazzling unrealities, or whether they are realities seized upon at a moment's glance, we leave his detractors and admirers to settle between them.'

That Turner's was a vision of reality was clear at least to another critic, William Makepeace Thackeray, whose account in the June number of *Fraser's Magazine* reflects in its ebullience what must have been the characteristic response of the average Cockney:

'As for Mr Turner, he has out-prodigied all former prodigies. He has made a picture with real rain, behind which is real sunshine, and you expect a rainbow every minute. Meanwhile there comes a train down upon you, really moving at the rate of fifty miles an hour, and which the reader had best make haste to see, lest it should dash out of the picture, and be away up Charing Cross through the wall opposite. All these wonders are performed with means not less wonderful than the effects are. The rain, in the astounding picture called "Rain – Steam – Speed", is composed of dabs of dirty putty *slapped* on to the canvas with a trowel; the sunshine scintillates out of very thick, smeary lumps of chrome yellow. The shadows are produced by cool tones of crimson lake, and quiet glazings of vermilion; although the fire in the steam-engine *looks* as if it were red, I am not prepared to say that it is not painted with cobalt and pea-green. And as for the manner in which the "*Speed*" is done, of that the less said the better – only it is a positive fact that there is a steam-coach going fifty miles an hour. The world has never seen anything like this picture.'

Turner was not the painter to invent a subject if he could borrow one from another artist, and the isolation of his railway theme among British landscapes of the period is remarkable. *Rain, Steam and Speed* can certainly be related to some of the illustrations of T. T. Bury [1] and J. W. Carmichael [2] (whose own style is itself clearly dependent upon Turnerian series like the *Southern Coast* and *England and Wales*, and may have been transmitted through their common engraver, J. T. Willmore); but although Turner sometimes used prints and illustrations as an *aide-memoire*, he does not seem ever to have made them the starting-point for a new type of

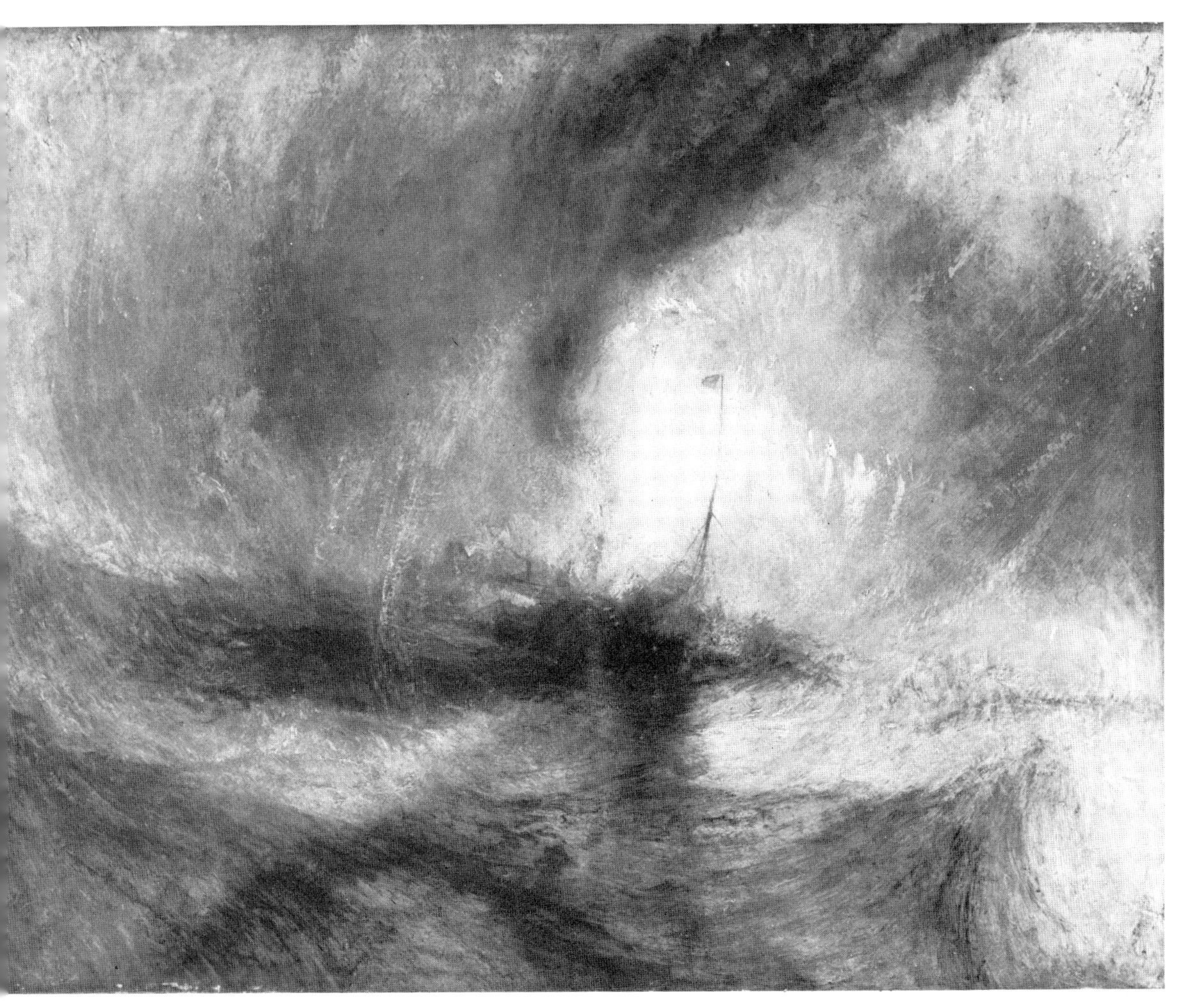

3. *Snowstorm*, 1842. J. M. W. Turner

subject, and it is very unlikely that he did so in this case. A story that is still often repeated has it that the picture, like the *Hannibal Crossing the Alps* of 1812, and the *Snowstorm: Steamboat off a Harbour's Mouth* of 1842 [3] in the Tate Gallery, London, was painted as the immediate result of a direct experience – in this case one which Turner shared with another passenger on the Railway, Lady Simon, who had joined the train at Exeter:

'In the coach seated opposite her [as she later told George Richmond] was an elderly gentleman, short and stout, with a red face and a curious, prominent nose. The weather was very wild, and by-and-by a violent storm swept over the country, blotting out the sunshine and the blue sky, and hanging like a pall over the landscape. The old gentleman seemed strangely excited at this, jumping up to open the window, craning his neck out, and finally calling to her to come and observe a curious effect of light. A train was coming in their direction, through the blackness, over one of Brunel's bridges, and the effect of the locomotive, lit by crimson flame, and seen through driving rain and whirling tempest, gave a peculiar impression of power, speed and stress.'

Some time afterwards Lady Simon was invited to the Academy Private View, and, 'In a flash she realised that the subject of the picture was what she had been called upon to admire out of the window of the coach'.[4]

This sense of *rapportage* is not inconsistent with a conception of landscape painting that Turner had upheld two years earlier in *Snowstorm* [3], in whose full title he had emphasized his own direct participation in the storm – *Snowstorm: steamboat off a Harbour's Mouth Making Signals in Shallow Water, and going by the Lead. The Author was in this storm on the night the Ariel left Harwich.*[5] But Lady Simon's account to George Richmond is full of impossibilities, and her better-known report to Ruskin is even more so. To Richmond she implied at one point, for example, that she and Turner had been together in a coach travelling to the station, rather than in the train itself which, in Turner's picture, is running

4. *Rain, Steam and Speed*, detail

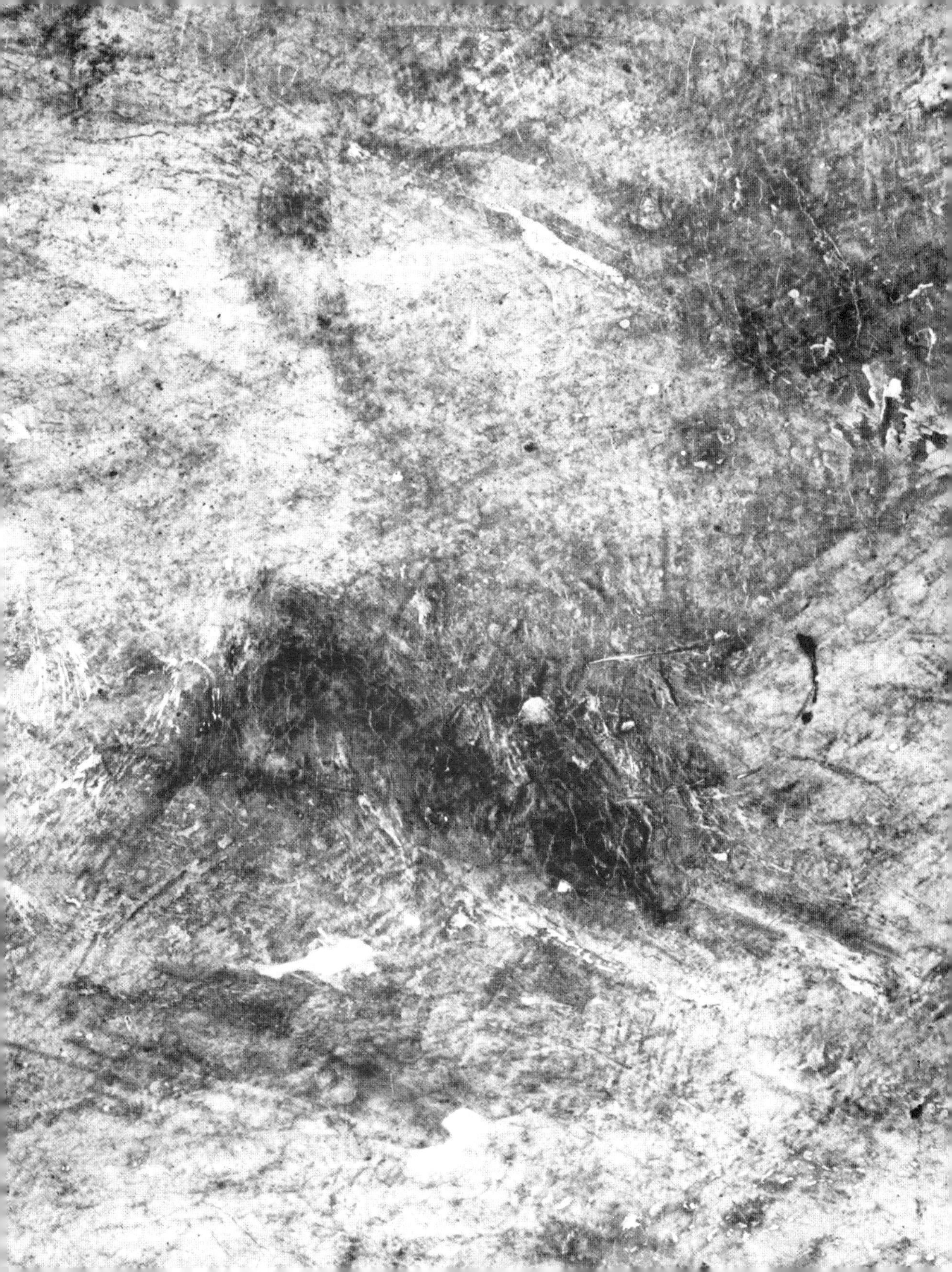

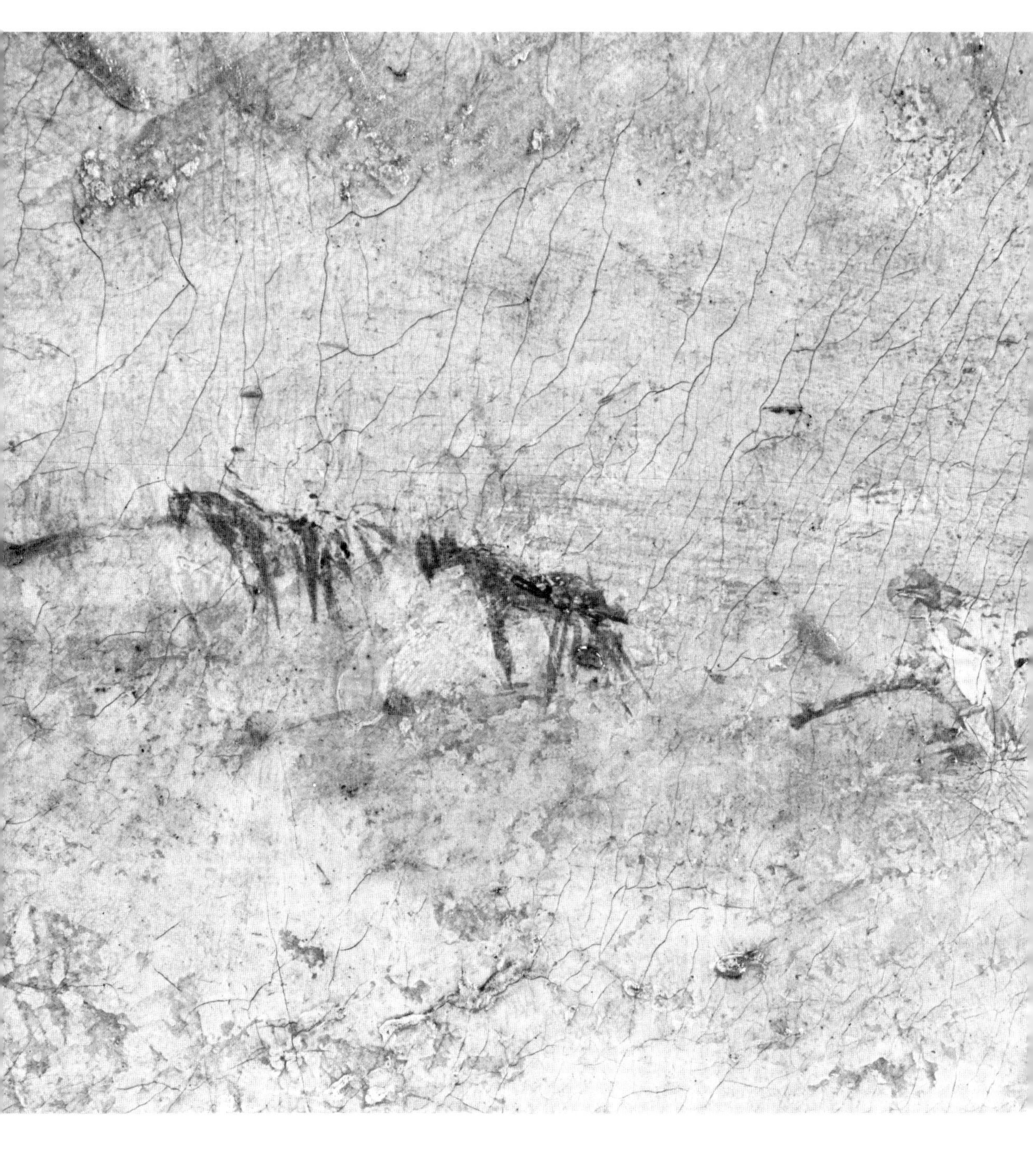

5. *Rain, Steam and Speed*, detail

on a single track line, and certainly cannot have been seen from a railway carriage passing in the opposite direction. Further, the road level at Maidenhead [12] is far below the bridge. For Ruskin's benefit the episode took place at night. But, whatever the circumstances of Turner's journey, and although the place recorded in his painting, Maidenhead Railway Bridge, is perfectly identifiable,[6] the picture is clearly no more the simple representation of a particular event than is *Hannibal*, which Turner had himself claimed went back to a storm he had witnessed in Yorkshire two years before the picture was exhibited.

Turner worked at *Rain, Steam and Speed* on the Academy wall during Varnishing Days, watched by the nine-year-old G. D. Leslie, who recalled many years later:

'He used rather short brushes, a very messy palette, and, standing very close up to the canvas, appeared to paint with his eyes and nose as well as his hand. Of course he repeatedly walked back to study the effect. Turner must, I think, have been fond of boys, for he did not seem to mind my looking on at him; on the contrary, he talked to me every now and then, and painted out the little hare running for its life in front of the locomotive on the viaduct [4]. This hare, and not the train, I have no doubt he intended to represent the "Speed" of his title; the word must have been in his mind when he was painting the hare, for close to it, on the plain below the viaduct, he introduced the figure of a man ploughing [5], "Speed the plough" (the name of an old country dance) probably passing through his brain.'[7]

As Leslie's account suggests, and as the title of the picture itself makes clear, Turner was painting not a view of the Great Western Railway, but an allegory of the forces of nature, cast in the form of a landscape of striking naturalism and immediacy, but none the less allegorical that its imagery was so modern. He was, indeed, updating a type of Baroque allegory with which he and his audience were only too familiar in, for example, Benjamin West's series of

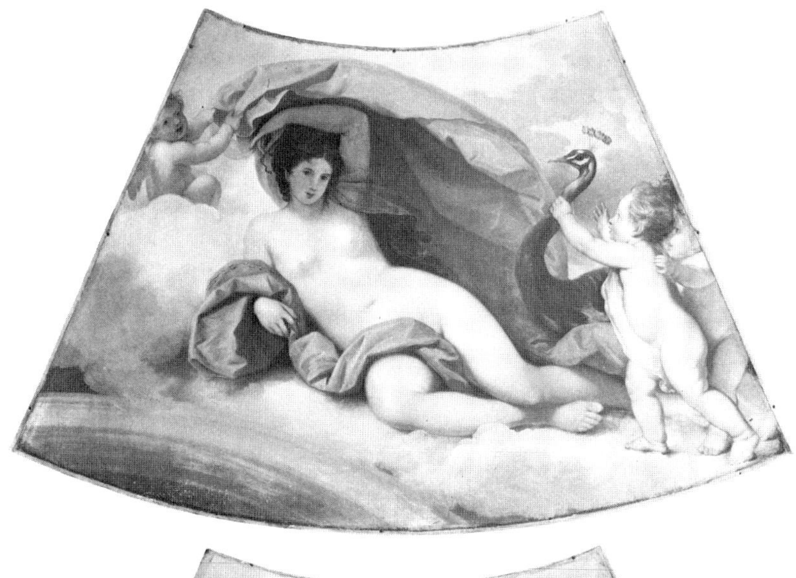

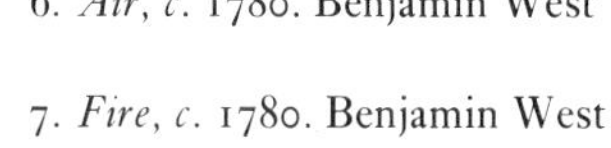

6. *Air, c.* 1780. Benjamin West

7. *Fire, c.* 1780. Benjamin West

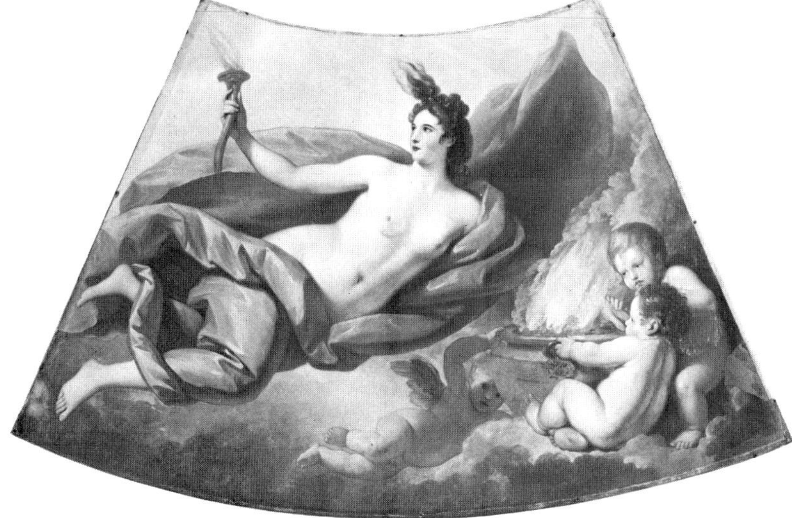

the *Four Elements* [6, 7] surrounding *The Graces Unveiling Nature* on the ceiling of the Royal Academy.[8]

Turner's painting can be related to a development in symbolic landscape, initiated in the 1810s with his *Battle Abbey; the Spot where Harold Fell* [8], in which he had used a similar image of a coursing hare.[9] And he had revived the same image more recently in a painting of the Ovidian story of *Apollo and Daphne* [9a, b]:

8 *(right)*. *Battle Abbey*, 1819.
J. M. W. Turner, engr. W. B. Cooke

9a *(below right)*. *Apollo and Daphne*, 1837. J. M. W. Turner

9b *(below)*. Detail of 9a

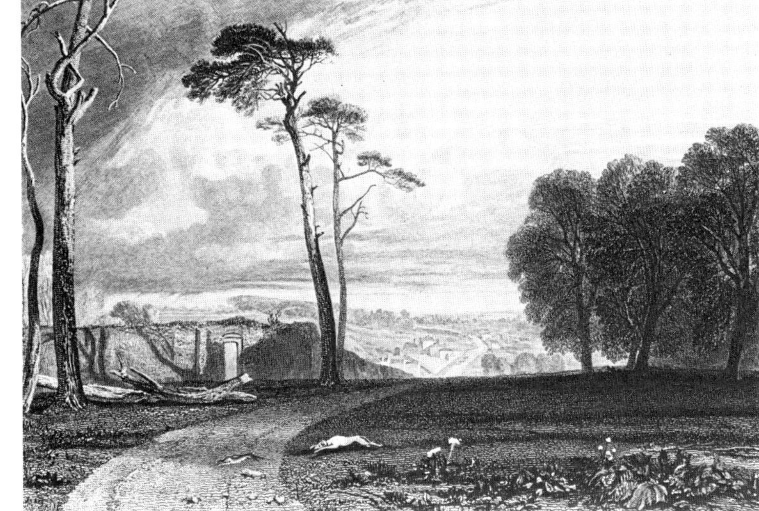

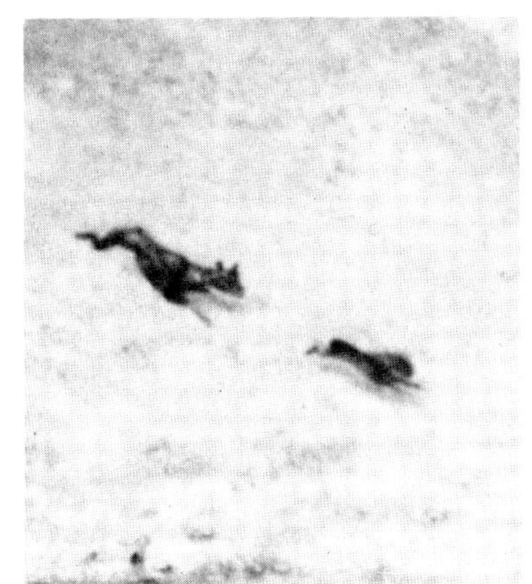

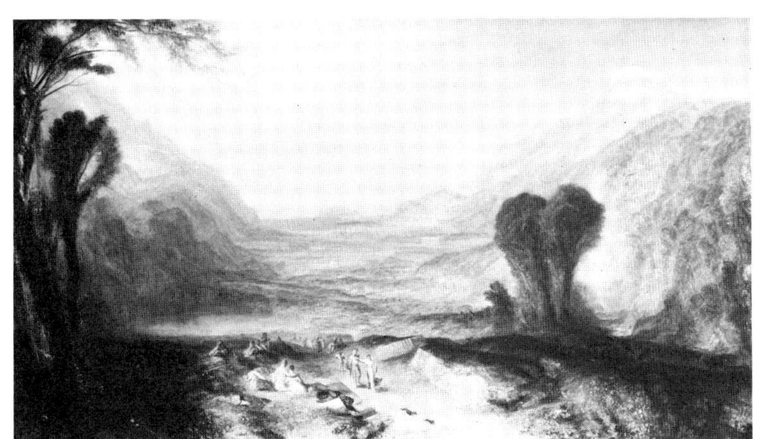

As when th' impatient greyhound, slipt from far,
Bounds o'er the glebe to course the fearful hare,
She, in her speed, does all her safety lay;
And he, with double speed, pursues the prey.

Hound and hare were for Turner the most characteristic emblems of speed; and, with his interest in the often fanciful names of the early locomotives, perhaps he knew that one of the engines of the

'Firefly' class, in use on the Great Western, the type he showed in his painting, was called *Greyhound*[10] [10, 11].

If the inception of Turner's picture cannot with certainty be understood in terms of a single specific event, the choice of the Great Western for its railway imagery was none the less far from haphazard, for the Great Western was the *doyen* of the railway

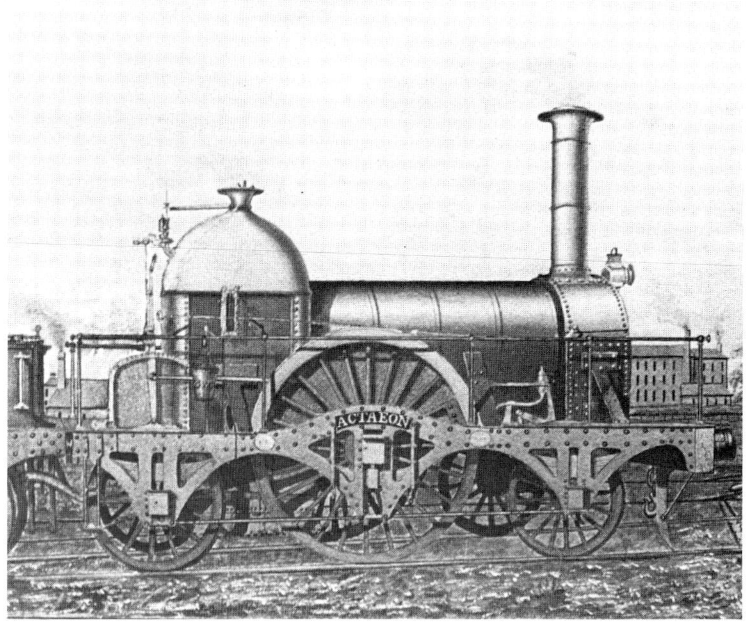

10. 'Firefly' Class Locomotive, *Actaeon*, 1841–55

11 *(right)*. *Rain, Steam and Speed*, detail

system: 'the most gigantic work', in the words of an early railway historian, 'not only in Great Britain, not only in Europe, but in the entire world.' By the beginning of 1845 it had a far greater mileage than any other railway (over 230 miles); and according to J. Francis, by virtue of its huge seven-foot gauge, 'the imaginative vision of the shareholders beheld Titanic arches and vast tunnels'; 'magnificent bridges and fine viaducts; and the hundred miles an hour prophesied by the engineer [Brunel], exceeded the narrow gauge to an extent which promised to compel a traffic'.[11] Turner chose as the setting for his motif one of Brunel's most 'magnificent

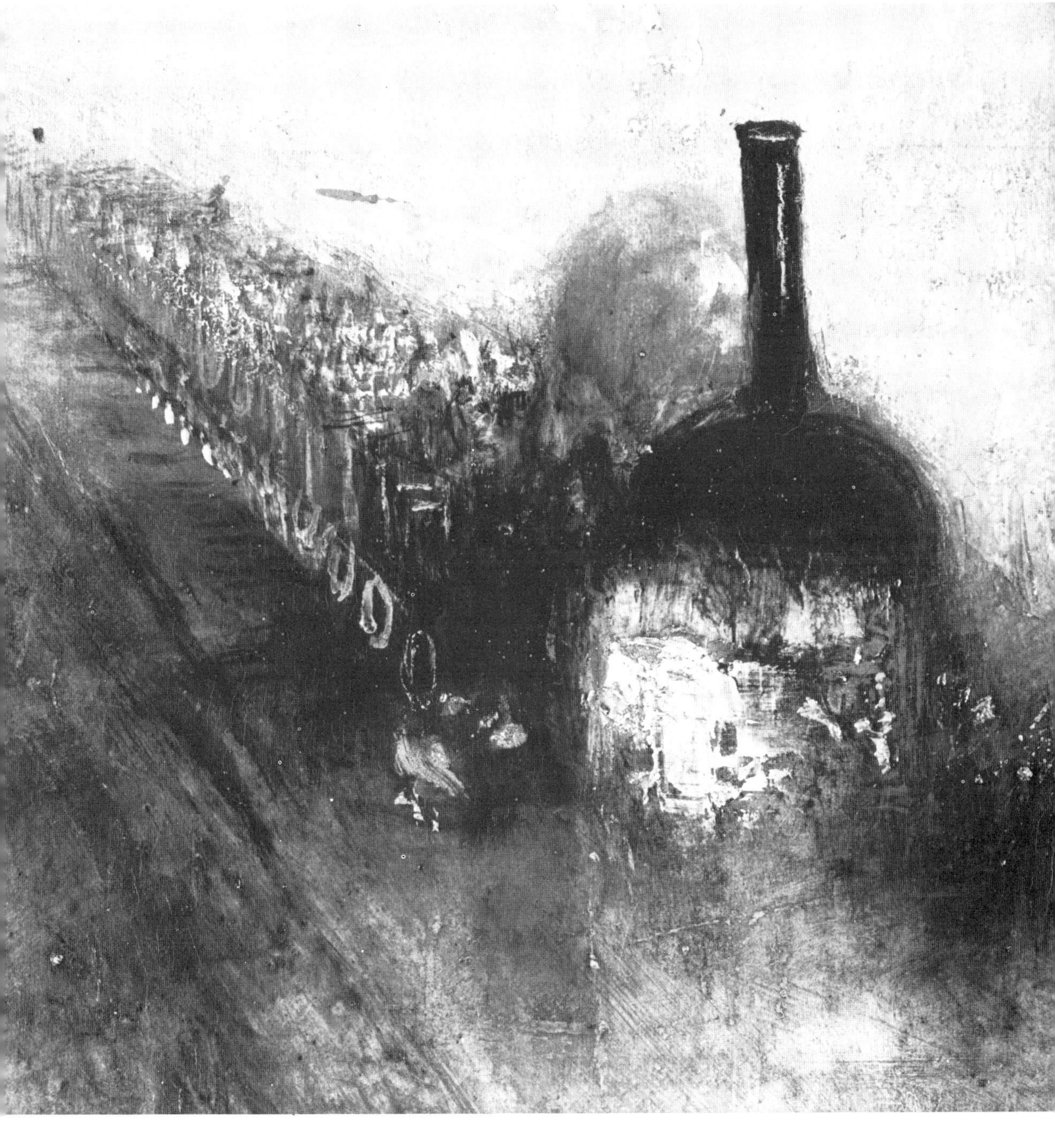

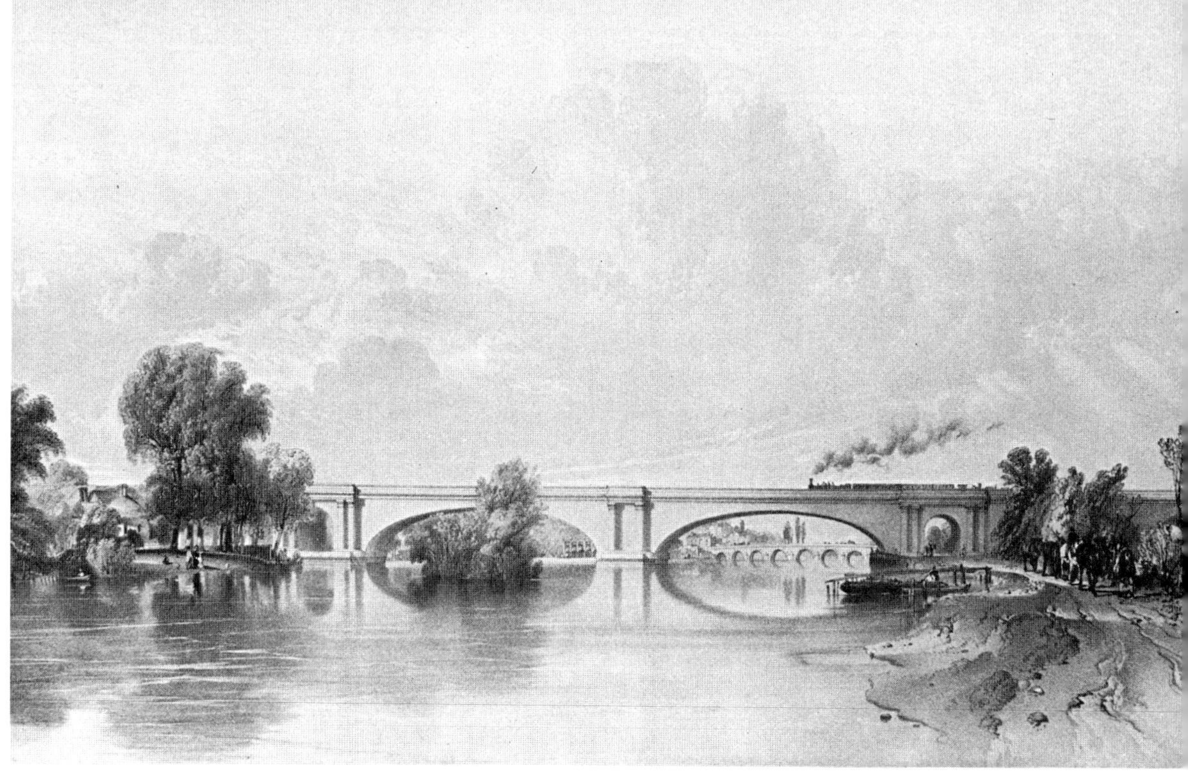

12. *Maidenhead Railway Bridge*, 1846. J. C. Bourne

bridges' [12], itself a triumph of engineering, with its two 130-foot flat elliptical arches, which critics had condemned to an early collapse when they were constructed in 1839.

'To the eye familiar with geometrical beauty, [wrote a Victorian guidebook],[12] the perfect execution of an elliptical arch, on so large a scale, and so high a degree of eccentricity, is an uncommon gratification; but when the practical mechanician considers the difficulties and risks which must have attended its construction . . . , then indeed, and only then, will he sufficiently appreciate the courage and the capacity which have approached so near the verge of possibility without transgressing its bounds.'

Maidenhead Bridge was set, too, amid that lush tract of Thames scenery that Turner had explored so lovingly for nearly thirty years [13, 14], and to whose beauties J. C. Bourne, in his magnificent guidebook to the Railway of 1846, was especially concerned to draw the attention of the traveller:

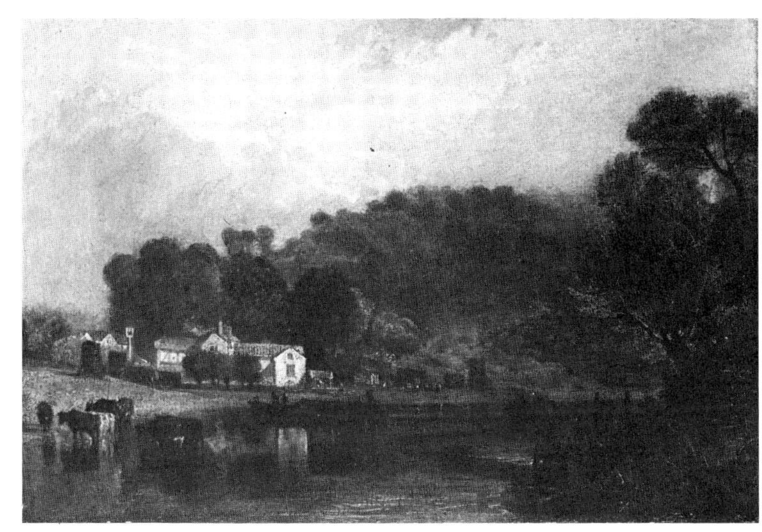

13 *(right)*. *Cliveden on Thames*, *c*. 1807. J. M. W. Turner

14. *View of the Thames*, *c*. 1807. J. M. W. Turner

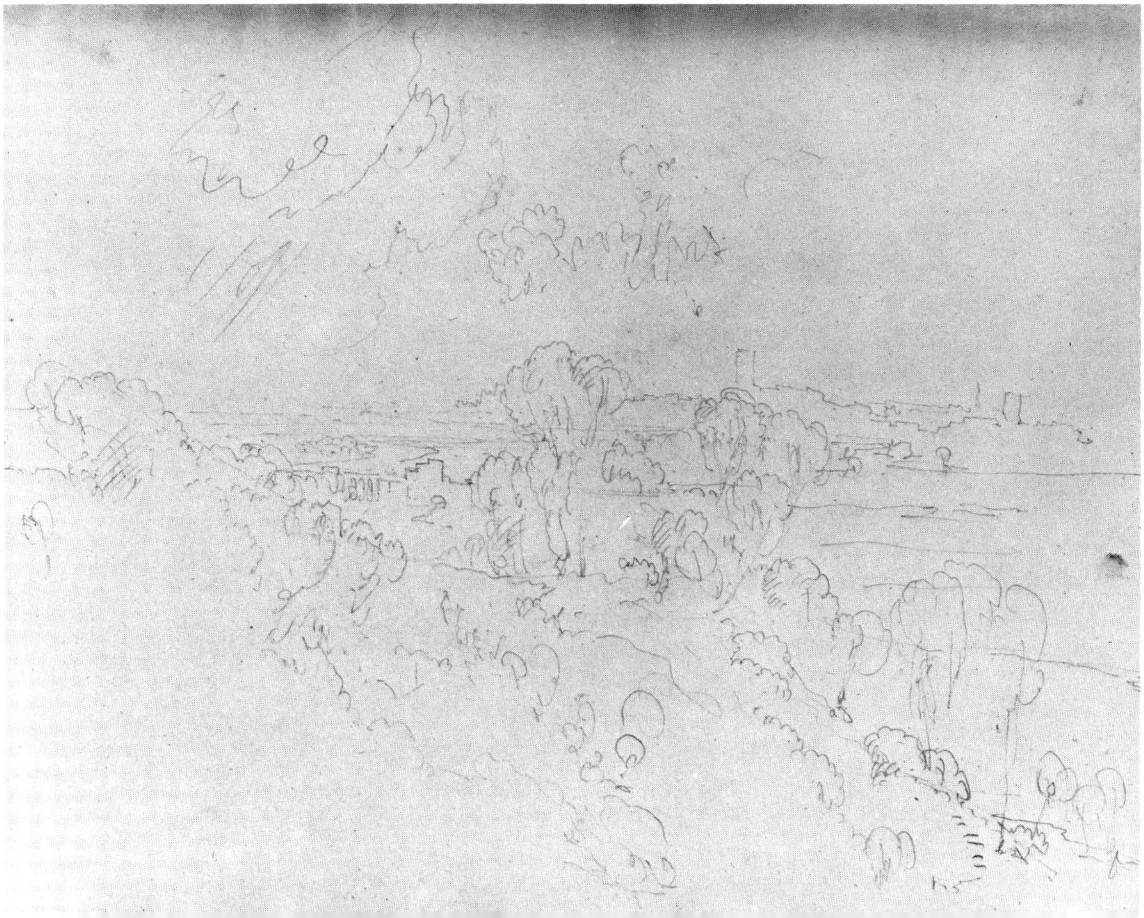

'The view from the bridge, both up and down the river is particularly fine. Upwards, in the foreground, is the old bridge, erected about 1780, from the designs of Sir Robert Taylor, and in the distance the hanging woods of Taplow and Cliefden, "With their beechen wreaths the king of rivers crowning" ascend from the margin of the stream, and terminate in the imposing façade of Cliefden House. The view in the opposite direction commands the river

"... Flowing
To Windsor-ward amain"

and extends over St Leonards and the castle, including much of the park.'[13]

It was a tract, Turner had said, that could show finer scenery along its banks than any river in Italy.[14] Moreover, the railway led, in the direction that Turner's train is travelling, to that other favourite hunting-ground of the Turnerian Picturesque, Devonshire, the setting of *Crossing the Brook* (Tate Gallery).[15] At the opening of the Bristol and Exeter line in 1844 it was not overlooked that the Great Western was bringing this Picturesque terrain closer to the tourist: *The Railway Times* pointed out that, 'it had been stated that in former times, though Devonshire was a most beautiful county, those beauties were not often seen by the stranger, in consequence of the lines of road chosen. Now there was a magnificent highway passing through the richest portion of the scenery . . .'[16]

Not only did the Great Western link regions of the English countryside that were closest to Turner's heart; it was a line that continued to be very much in the public eye. Prince Albert had chosen it for his first journey by rail in November 1839, from Slough to Paddington; and he had persuaded the Queen to venture on the same journey three years later. In July 1843 the Prince had travelled to Bristol by train, to launch Brunel's steamship *Great Britain*, and on the return journey had made the excellent time of two hours forty minutes.[17]

Although the average speed on the Great Western of 33 m.p.h. in 1844 was only the second fastest in the country, speed was indeed one of its foremost claims as a service (Brunel had prophesied 100 m.p.h.), and a year after Turner's picture, it introduced the fastest service ever with expresses travelling at an average speed of 43 m.p.h.[18]

'Now the railway system outstripped every speed that had ever been heard of before [wrote Bourne] and it did this at once. . . . Five years ago, no man had ever travelled from London to Bristol, even by the mail, in much less than twelve hours; upon the opening of the railway the distance was performed in four hours; and, more recently, parts of the road have been travelled over at a speed of fifty and sixty miles in the hour.'[19]

On 18 March 1844 *The Times*, under the headline 'Race with a Railway Engine', recorded an involuntary race between an Indian Officer-Cadet's thoroughbred and a locomotive at Ware in Hertfordshire, in which the bolting horse was run down. The railway had indeed become a byword for speed; and Turner's locomotive has something of the quality of an emblem or an illustrated proverb. 'Our very language begins to be affected', wrote a commentator. 'Men talk of "getting up the steam", of "railway speed", and reckon distances by hours and minutes.'[20] Turner may well have taken a direct interest in these developments on the Great Western in particular, for in 1841 his friend John Martin, from whom he seems to have borrowed a theme or two in these years,[21] had travelled on the footplate with Brunel in speed trials between Southall and Slough, in which the locomotive is said to have touched 90 m.p.h.[22]

And yet it is significant that it was Turner and not Martin who turned the experience into the subject of a painting, for Martin, although he was a civil engineer directly involved in the Industrial Revolution, felt that it had little to offer the artist. If we are to follow some recent critics in imagining a technological background to Martin's apocalyptic visions of *The Destruction of Sodom*, *The Deluge*, *The Fall of Niniveh*, or *Milton's Pandemonium*, it is clear that in his mind this technology could only be associated with cataclysm and disaster; and in this Martin reflected a widely-felt Romantic abhorrence of the Railway Age. The fear had already been voiced in Parliament in the 1830s:

'The whole country was to be traversed and dissected by iron roads. Wherever there was a hamlet or a cattle track, a market or a manufactory, there was to be a railroad; physical objects and private rights were straws under the chariot wheels of the Fire King. Mountains were to be cut through; valleys were to be lifted; the skies were to be scaled; the earth was to be tunnelled; parks, gardens and ornamental grounds were to be broken into; the shrieking engine was to carry the riot of the town into the sylvan retreats of pastoral life; sweltering trains were to penetrate solitudes hitherto sacred to the ruins of antiquity; hissing locomotives were to rush over the tops of houses . . .'[23]

It was this other, darker side of the Railway Revolution which seems most to have engaged the poets and novelists of the period. Wordsworth, who had welcomed the images, if not the realities, of the technological age in his Preface of 1801 to the *Lyrical Ballads*, and in 1833, at the beginning of the railway developments, had extended a lukewarm hand to their ugly products in a sonnet, 'Steamboats, Viaducts and Railways', hardened into opposition when, ten years later, he saw his Lakeland solitude threatened by a proposed Kendal and Windermere Railway. In the year of *Rain, Steam and Speed*, he asked,

> Is there no nook of English ground secure
> From rash assault?

and concluded another sonnet to the mountains, written as part of an extended polemic conducted in the London *Morning Post* (see Appendix):

Now, for your shame, a Power, the Thirst of Gold
That rules o'er Britain like a baneful star,
Wills that your peace, your beauty, shall be sold,
And clear way made for her triumphal car
Through the beloved retreats your arms enfold!
Hear ye that whistle? As her long-linked Train
Swept onwards, did the vision cross your view?
Yes, ye were startled; and, in balance true,
Weighing the mischief with the promised gain,
Mountains, and Vales, and Floods, I call on you
To share the passion of a just disdain.

(*Miscellaneous Sonnets* XLV, XLVI)

Wordsworth's turgidly stated sentiments were endorsed by Ruskin, who was at this very moment proclaiming Turner's realism in the first volume of *Modern Painters*, where he laid it down that 'if we are to do anything great, good, awful, religious, it must be got out of our own little island, and out of this year 1846, railroads and all'. But in the second volume he quoted and echoed Wordsworth's fears, and when, many years later, the Lakes Railway was again an issue, he wrote a bitter pamphlet condemning it. So far from opening the countryside to new experience of the Picturesque, as had been claimed by the apologists, rail travel was closed to everything human. "Going by railway [he said] I do not consider as travel at all; it is merely being "sent" to a place, and very little different from becoming a parcel.'[24] And in all his lengthy commentaries on Turner's work, moving from an extreme naturalistic to an equally extreme symbolic posture in the later volumes of *Modern Painters*, he never once discussed *Rain, Steam and Speed*.

A Romantic horror of the railway as a powerful and wayward monster was also voiced in the eighteen forties by the only novelist who seems to have taken it seriously: Charles Dickens, who in *Dombey and Son*, presented it as an archetypal image of Death. Dombey, brooding in a train on his son's death, 'found no pleasure or relief in the journey. Tortured by these thoughts he carried monotony with him, through the rushing landscape, and hurried headlong, not through a rich and varied country, but a wilderness of blighted plans and gnawing jealousies. The very speed at which the train was whirled along mocked the swift course of the young life that had been born away so steadily and so inexorably to its fore-doomed end. The power that forced itself upon its iron way – its own – defiant of all paths and roads, piercing through the heart of every obstacle, and dragging living creatures of all classes, ages, and degrees behind it, was a type of the triumphant monster, Death.

'Away, with a shriek, and a roar, and a rattle, from the town, burrowing among the dwellings of men and making the streets hum, flashing out into the meadows for a moment, mining in through the damp earth, booming on in darkness and heavy air, bursting out again into the sunny day so bright and wide; away, with a shriek and a roar, and a rattle, through the fields, through the woods, through the corn, through the hay, through the chalk, through the mould, through the clay, through the rock, among objects close at hand and almost in the grasp, ever flying from the traveller, and a deceitful distance ever moving slowly within him; like as in the track of the remorseless monster, Death!

'Through the hollow, on the height, by the heath, by the orchard, by the park, by the garden, over the canal, across the river, where the sheep are feeding, where the mill is going, where the barge is floating, where the dead are lying, where the factory is smoking, where the stream is running, where the village clusters, where the great cathedral rises, where the bleak moor lies, and the wild breeze smoothes or ruffles it at its inconstant will; away, with a shriek, and a roar, and a rattle, and no trace to leave behind but dust and vapour; like the track of the remorseless monster, Death!

'Breasting the wind and light, the shower and sunshine, away, and still away, it rolls and roars, fierce and rapid, smooth and certain, and great works and massive bridges crossing up above,

15. Frontispiece to *Dombey and Son*, 1846. Phiz

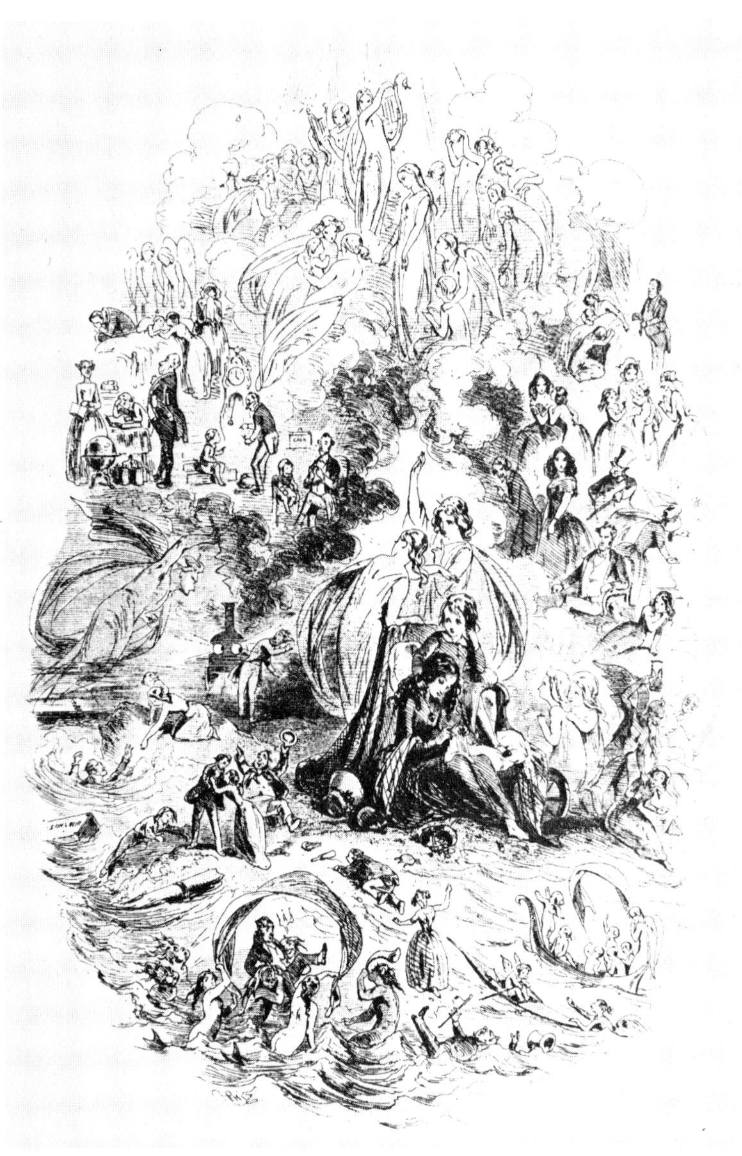

fall like a beam of shadow an inch broad upon the eye, and then are lost. Away, and still away, onward and onward ever; glimpses of cottage-homes, of houses, mansions, rich estates, of husbandry and handicraft, of people, of old roads and paths that look deserted, small, and insignificant as they are left behind; and so they do, and what else is there but such glimpses, in the track of the indomitable monster, Death!

'Away, with a shriek, and a roar, and a rattle, plunging down into the earth again, and working on in such a storm of energy and perseverance, that amidst the darkness and whirlwind the motion seems reversed, and to tend furiously backward, until a ray of light upon the wet wall shows its surface flying past like a fierce stream. Away once more into the day, and through the day, with a shrill yell of exultation, roaring, rattling, tearing on, spurning everything with its dark breath, sometimes pausing for a minute where a crowd of faces are, that in a minute more are not; sometimes lapping water greedily, and before the spout at which it drinks has ceased to drip upon the ground, shrieking, roaring, rattling through the purple distance! . . .' (Chapter XX).

The railway was also, in a form that is thoroughly reminiscent of Turner's image, the death of the villainous Mr Carker at the end of the novel:

'A trembling of the ground, and quick vibration in his ears; a distant shriek; a dull light advancing, quickly changed to two red eyes, and a fierce fire, dropping glowing coals; an irresistible bearing on of a great roaring and dilating mass; a high wind, and a rattle . . . looked round – saw the red eyes, bleared and dim in the daylight, close upon him – was beaten down, caught up, and whirled away upon a jagged mill, that spun him round and round, and struck him limb from limb, and licked his stream of life up with its fiery heat, and cast his mutilated fragments in the air . . .' (Chapter LV).

Perhaps not only Dickens, but also his illustrator 'Phiz' (H. K. Browne) took a cue from Turner. Browne's complex vignette for the frontispiece to *Dombey and Son* [15] surely owes something to Turner's figurative illustrations of the thirties to poems by Samuel Rogers and Thomas Campbell; and Browne had trained under one of Turner's engravers, William Finden, and was the brother-in-law of one of the painter's late patrons, Elhanan Bicknell.

But whatever its influence, later in the century, when Ruskin was expounding the dark significance of Turner's dying years, an apocalyptic symbolism similar to Dickens's was extracted from *Rain, Steam and Speed*. In his *History of Romanticism*, Théophile Gautier described the picture as 'a real cataclysm. Flashes of lightning, wings like great fire-birds, towering columns of cloud collapsing under the thunderbolts, rain whipped into vapour by the wind. You would have said it was the setting for the end of the world. Through all this writhed the engine, like the Beast of the Apocalypse, opening its red glass eyes in the shadows, and dragging after it, in a huge tail, its vertebrae of carriages.'[25]

Similarly, in England, Cosmo Monkhouse, in a late edition of the first collection of engravings to reproduce the picture, *The Turner Gallery*, pointed to

'the terror of the poor hare, who will surely be overtaken and crushed in an instant. Some persons see a deeper meaning in this picture, something analogous to that of the *Téméraire* (National Gallery) – the old order changing, the easy going past giving way to the quick-living future; and there is something in the contrast between the plough and the steam engine, the ugly form of the railway-bridge and train, and the beauty and peace of the old bridge and the landscape, which shows that some such thoughts were not absent from the painter's mind . . .'[26]

And yet there is nothing to suggest that Turner felt that the train and bridge were ugly; he painted in the hare jocularly as an emblem of speed, and no hare was likely to be outpaced by any locomotive of this period. The crowd of waving figures on the river-bank [16] reminds us that the railway was still a festive and popular entertainment. When the Bristol and Exeter line was opened on 1 May 1844, all business in Exeter was suspended and tens of thousands of people flocked in from the country to throng

16. *Rain, Steam and Speed*, detail

the streets, with bands playing. In 1836 the Hampshire clergy had petitioned against the railways, 'because the rustics kept away from church to see the trains pass by'.[27] The railway excursion became a major form of holiday attraction for the people, reaching the scale of a medieval pilgrimage. On 9 April 1844, after Easter Monday, *The Times* reported:

'In pursuance of advertisements which have appeared in most of the newspapers announcing cheap excursions by the Brighton Railway, long before 8 o'clock yesterday morning a great concourse of persons, dressed in their holiday attire, assembled at the terminus by London-bridge. By 8 o'clock the crowd at the office doors was so great, that the secretary sent to the M division station-house for the assistance of some of the police. Accordingly sergeants Woodhouse and Havill attended, and assisted the railway police in keeping the pressure of the crowd from the office doors. The passengers were then admitted to the clerks' desks in batches of 20 at a time.

'At half-past 8 o'clock the first train for Brighton started, with 30 carriages containing 900 persons; which were propelled by four engines, each party having purchased excursion tickets. In the course of the day six other trains left the terminus, carrying in the whole during the day 2,500 passengers. Not an accident of any kind happened during the day. The passengers by the Brighton train were, for the most part, mechanics and their wives. The reporter was informed last night by a guard of one of the return-trains that Brighton was so full of company, that lodgings could not be procured in the town, and at the outskirts the people were making a rich harvest by exacting from 5s to 10s for a single bed; provisions were also of a corresponding price.'

There is nothing to suggest that Turner was not thoroughly in sympathy with these developments. Brought up in the 1790s in contact with the industrial landscapist P. J. de Loutherbourg, he had always taken industrial motifs in his stride; and by 1800 had already produced in watercolour some masterpieces in the *genre*

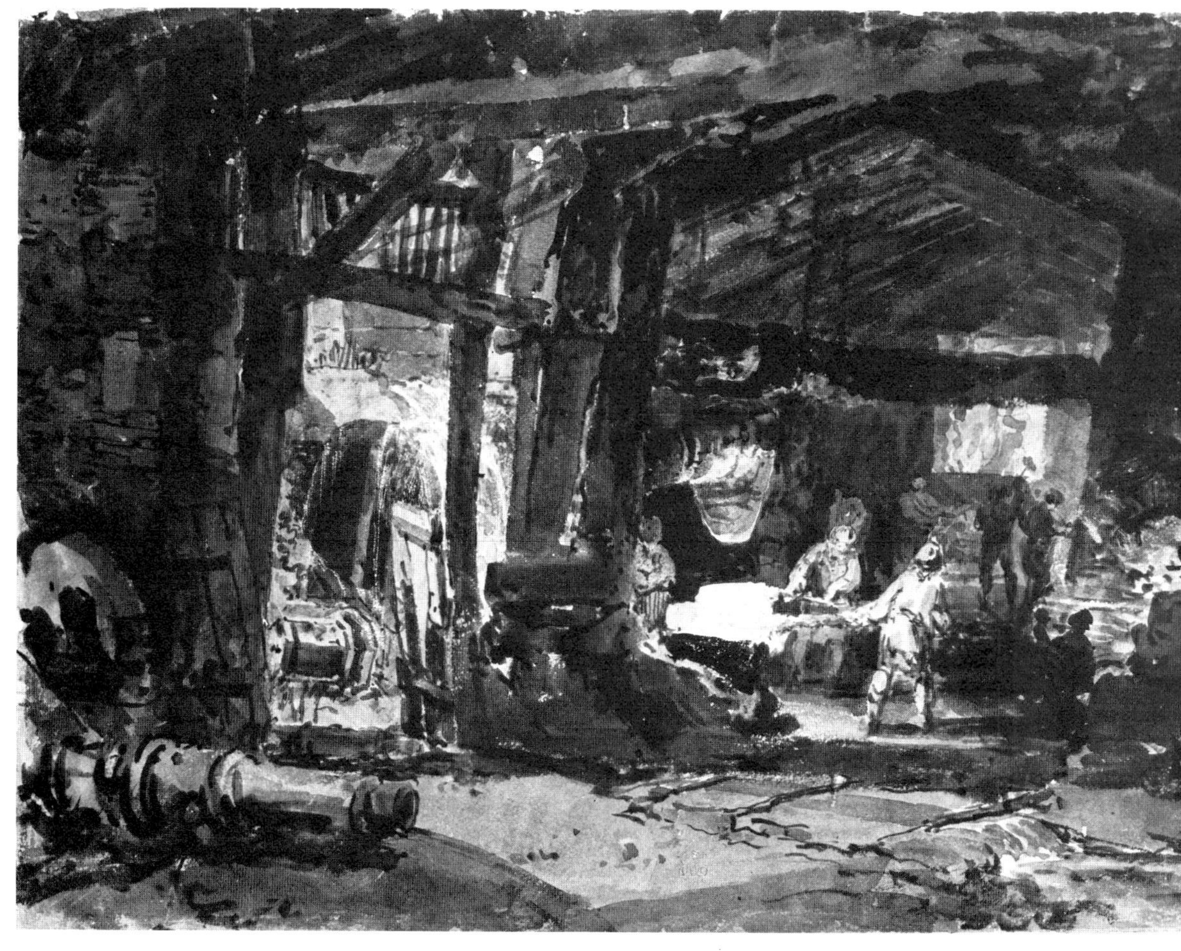

[17].[28] Turner also seems to have been interested in this type of subject on a monumental scale: the large canvas exhibited in 1847 as *The Hero of a Hundred Fights* [18] was repainted on a factory scene originally done about 1800. Furthermore, as an inveterate traveller from his early teens, Turner became obsessed with the problems and the delights of transport, to which he brought an extraordinary relish. One of his early *Oxford Almanack* drawings, *Oxford from Headington Hill* [19], is as much a celebration of coaching as it is of the city; and two of his Alpine crossings, in 1820 and

17 *(left). An Iron Foundry, c.* 1797. J. M. W. Turner

18 *(right). The Hero of a Hundred Fights, c.* 1800–1847. J. M. W. Turner

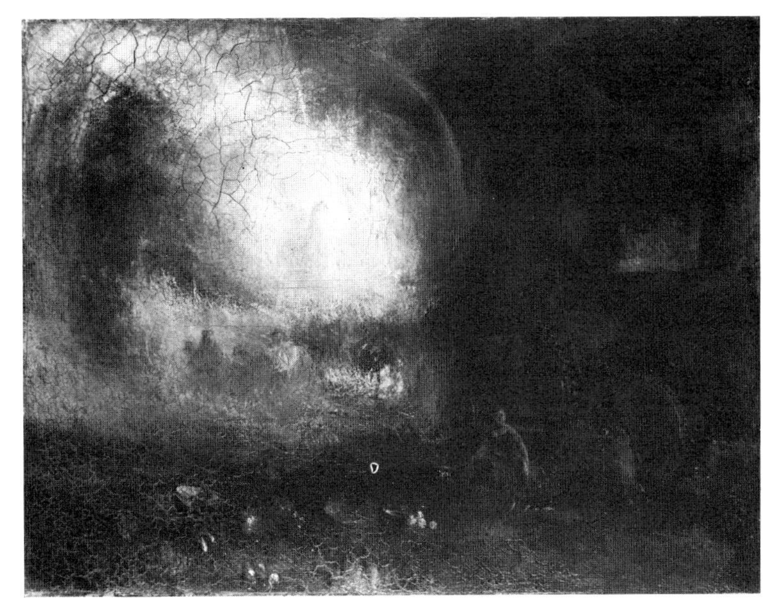

19. *Oxford from Headington Hill,* 1803–4. J. M. W. Turner

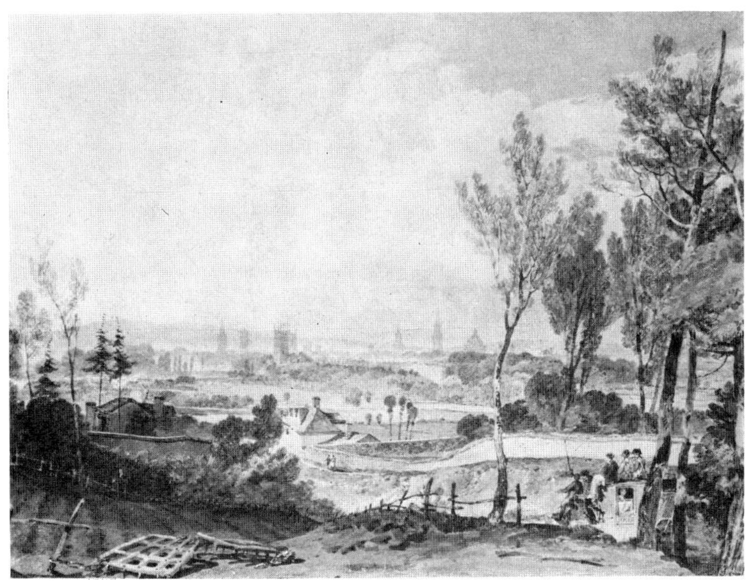

1829, he recorded in brilliant watercolours [20, 21], the second of which, *Messieurs les Voyageurs in a Snowdrift*, he saw fit to exhibit at the Academy. That these experiences were especially close to Turner's heart is suggested by the detailed and exuberant accounts he gave of each of them in letters to friends:

'Mont Cenis has been closed for some time [he wrote in January 1826 to James Holworthy], tho' the papers say some hot-headed Englishman did venture to cross *à pied* a month ago, and what they considered there madness to attempt, which honour was conferred once on me and my companion *de voiture*. We were capsized on the top [20]. Very lucky it was so; and the carriage door so completely frozen that we were obliged to get out at the window – the guide and Cantoniers began to fight, and the driver was by a process verbal put into prison, so doing while we had to march or rather flounder up to our knees, nothing less, in snow, all the way down to Lancesbyburgh [sc. Lanslebourg] by the King of Roadmaker's Road, not the Colossus of Roads, Mr MacAdam, but Bonaparte, filled up by snow and only known by the precipitous zig-zag . . .'[29]

Of the crossing in January 1829 he concluded a letter to Charles Lock Eastlake:

'Now for my journey *home*. Do not think any poor devil ever had such another, but quite satisfactory for one thing at least, viz. not to be so late in the season of winter again, for the snow began to fall at Foligno, tho' more of ice than snow, that the coach from its weight slide [*sic*] about in all directions, that walking was much preferable, but my innumerable tails would not do that service, so I soon got wet through and through, till at Sarre-valli [sc. Serrevalle] the diligence zizd into a ditch, and required 6 oxen, sent three miles back for, to drag it out; this cost 4 Hours, that we were 10 Hours beyond our time at Macerata, consequently half starved and frozen we at last got to Bologna . . . But there our troubles began

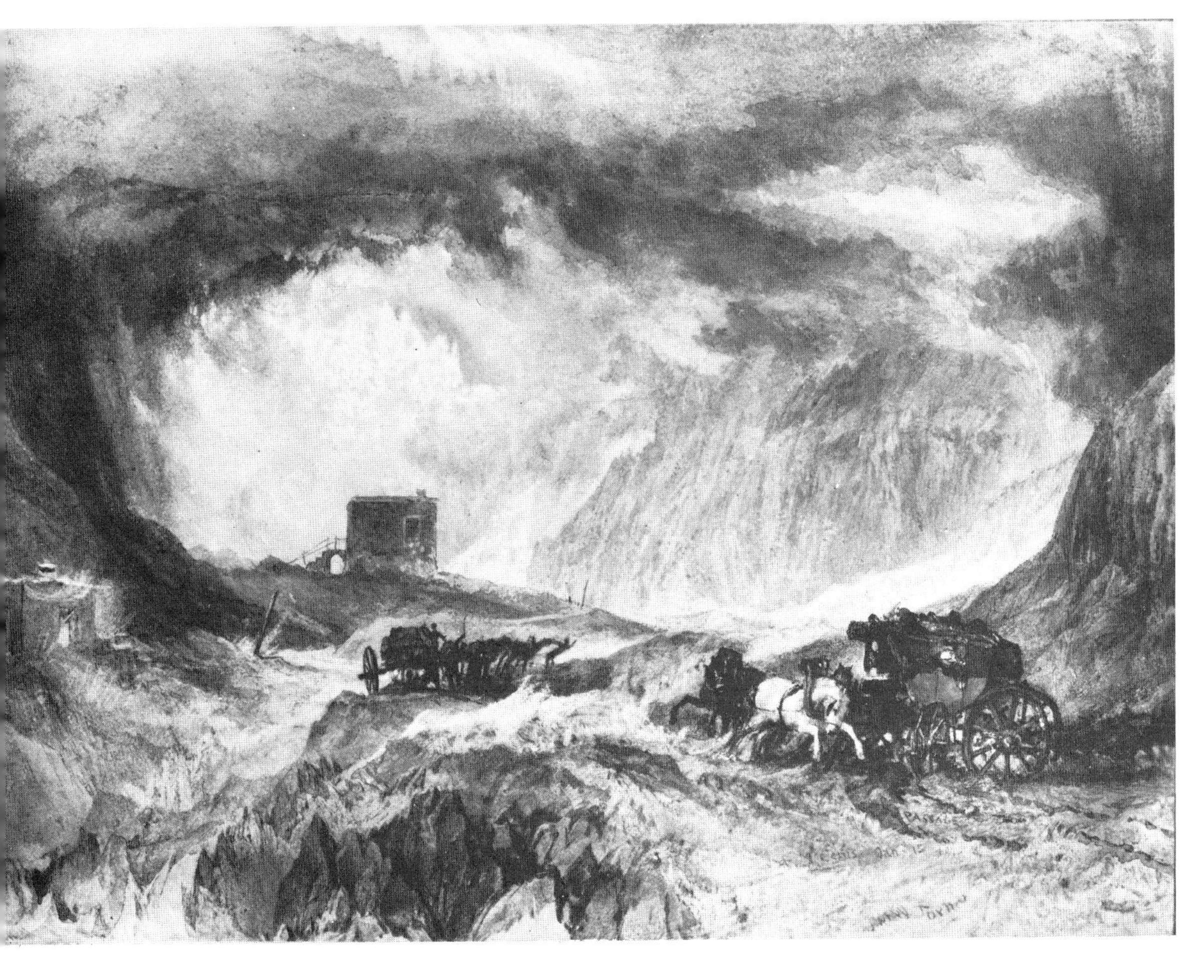

20. *Snowstorm, Mont Cenis*, 1820. J. M. W. Turner

instead of diminishing – the Milan diligence was unable to pass Placentia [sc. Piacenza]. We therefore hired a voitura, the horses were knocked up the first post, Sigr. turned us over to another, lighter carriage, which put my coat in full requisition night and day, for we never could keep warm or make our day's distance good. The places we put up at proved all bad till Firenzola being even the worst, for the down diligence people had devoured everything eatable (Beds none) . . . crossed Mont Cenis on a sledge – bivouacked

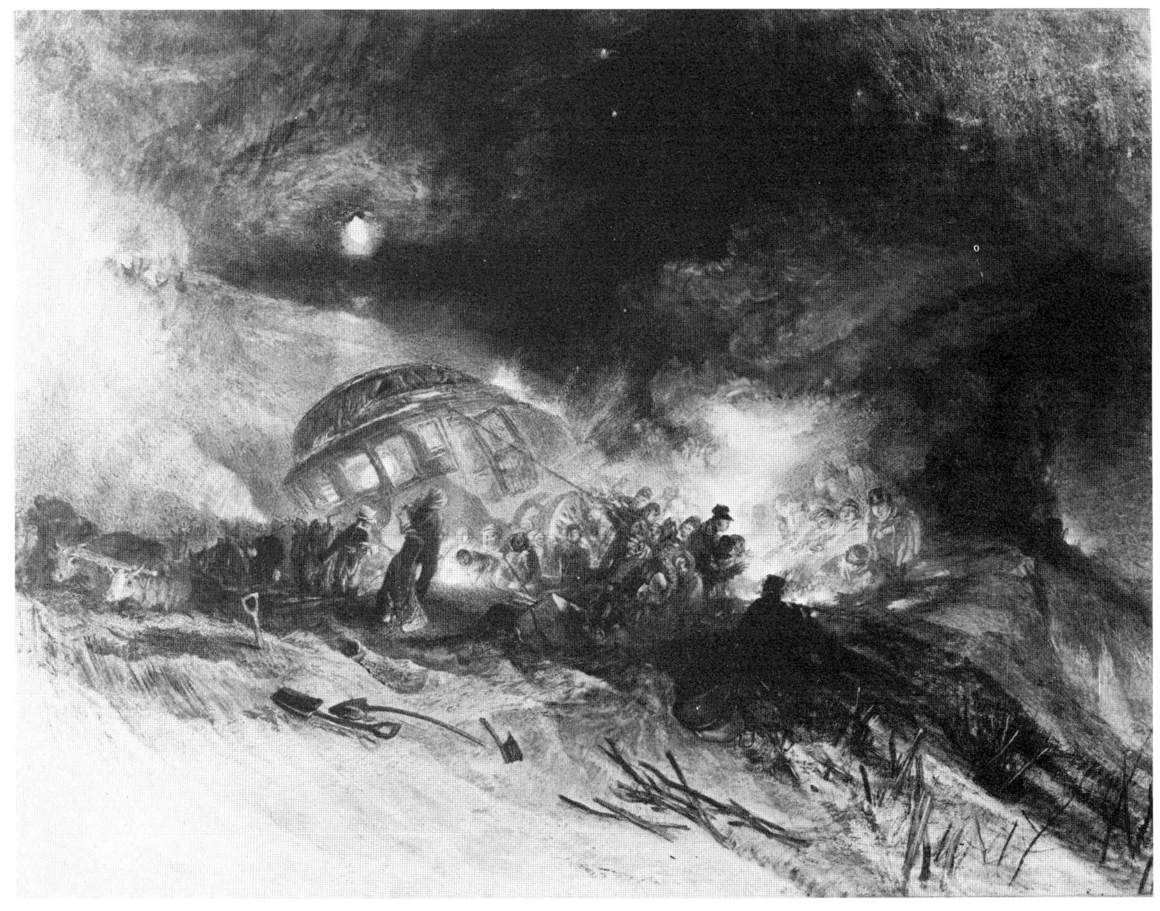

21. *Messieurs les Voyageurs in a Snowdrift*, 1829. J. M. W. Turner

in the snow with fires lighted for 3 Hours on Mont Tarate while the diligence was righted and dug out [21], for a Bank of Snow saved it from upsetting – and in the same night we were again turned out to walk up to our knees in new fallen drift to get assistance to dig a channel thro' it for the coach, so that from Foligno to within 20 miles of Paris I never saw the road but snow.'[30]

Coaching had long been for Turner a method of gathering material; many sketchbook pages record the passing panorama like a sheet of shorthand writing, and often, in their indecipherability, bear witness to the terrible condition of the roads themselves [22].

But as he grew older, sheer visual memory increasingly replaced even this shorthand, and we know of no preliminary material either for the *Snowstorm* of 1842 [3] or for *Rain, Steam and Speed.* Many of Turner's most characteristic marines, *Calais Pier* (Tate Gallery); *Harbour of Dieppe (changement de domicile)*; *Cologne, the Arrival of a Packet-boat* (both in the Frick Collection, New York); *Now for the Painter* (in Manchester City Gallery), are essentially pictures of

22. *On the Route through Savoy,* 1820. J. M. W. Turner

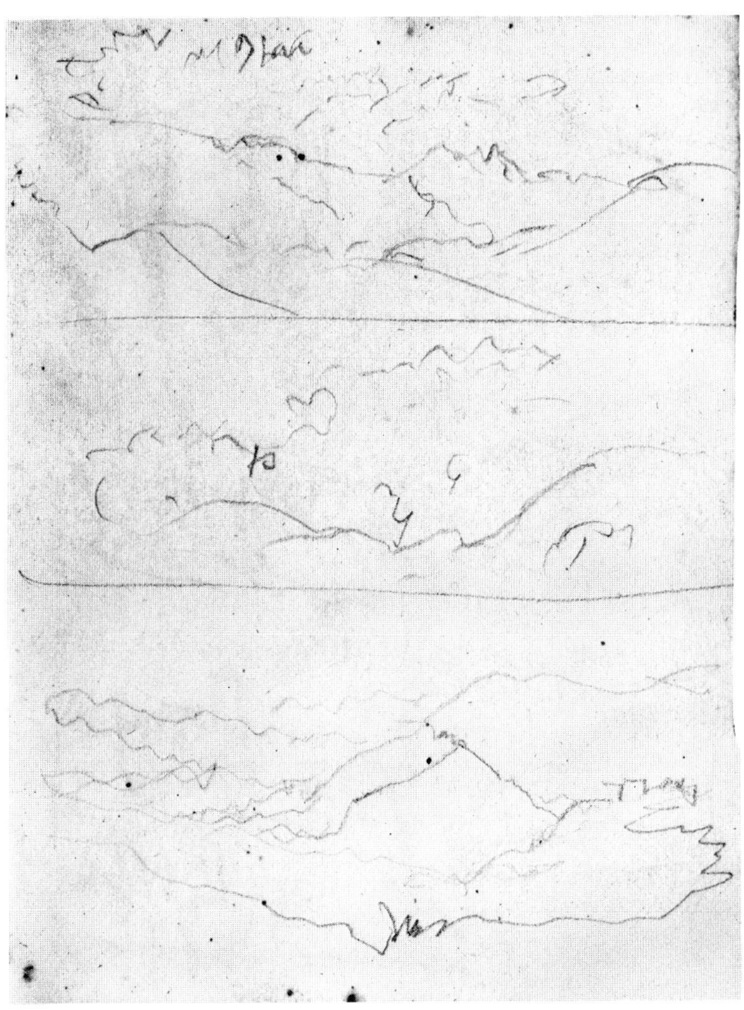

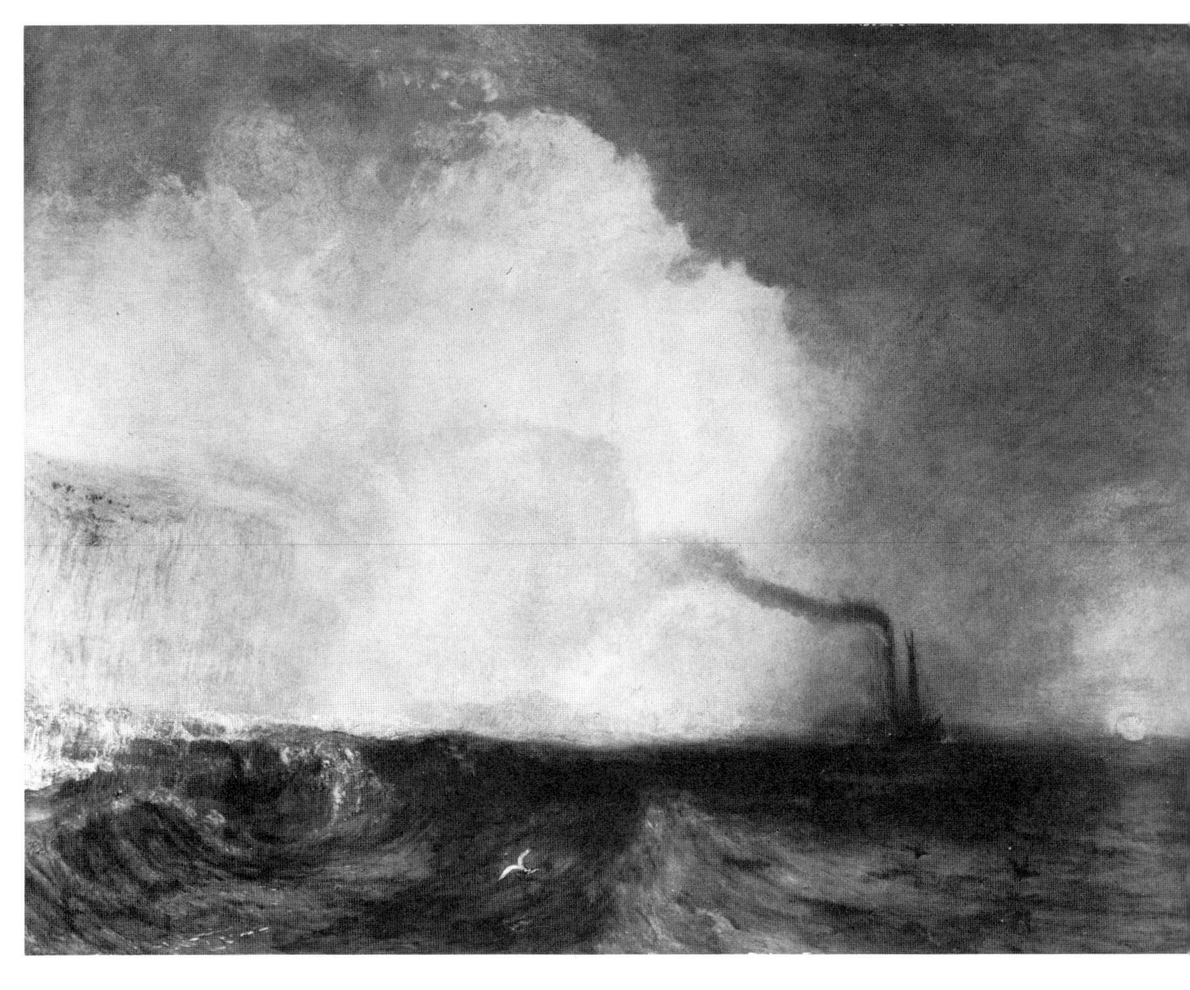

23. *Staffa: Fingal's Cave*, 1832. J. M. W. Turner

travel; and the Age of Steam brought little change of emphasis. *Staffa: Fingal's Cave* [23] and *Snowstorm: Steamboat off a Harbour's Mouth* [3] use the potential of the new imagery to tell a story of the painter's journeys in a way exactly analogous to *Rain, Steam and Speed*, and in each case he underlined his personal involvement in a vivid verbal record.[31] Turner returned so repeatedly to the sites in Britain and abroad which he had made the material of his painting, that we feel he wanted to travel as much as to arrive: technology simply extended what was an old and ingrained pre-occupation.

Although he left no records of his journeys on the Great Western, Turner certainly felt and shared the general excitement about the railway and railway travel. In an ebullient, if opaque, note of 1840 to his solicitor, George Cobb of Brighton, Turner showed that he would have shared the enjoyments of the London working-class:

'. . . having locomotive Engines in Progress towards you, we may meet again ere long – by rail-road, either at Brighton or London, but I suppose you are not so located by the heels, Mr Jack of Trumps, but do come to town occasionally, by the Rapid Dart or Quicksilver: that I do hope to see you before the Chemin de Fer is completed.'[32]

A peculiarly extravagant patron, the Birmingham pen-manufacturer Joseph Gillot, Turner referred to perfectly naturally as a 'Comet'.[33] He quickly absorbed the railway ethos into a system already highly sensitive to the seductions of travel; and it was perhaps inevitable that he should capitalize upon its peculiar immediacy in his pictorial imagery of power. But equally inevitably, he could not leave the engine in *Rain, Steam and Speed* to speak entirely for itself. In his search for the explicit, he produced a picture which, like much else in Turner, hovers between the poetic and the banal. It is a sign of his weakness as well as of his strength that subsequent spectators lost the banality of the imagery in the poetry of an all but incomparable pictorial technique.

2. Turner and Rembrandt

If, in his endeavour to redeem his subject from any suggestion of ambiguity, Turner drew on a type of symbolic imagery that is essentially Baroque, this is no less the case with the brilliant formal idiom in which his conception was clothed. In the tightly interwoven, centrally planned, two-dimensional composition of *Snowstorm: Steamboat off a Harbour's Mouth* [3], where the distant boat has been pulled to the surface of the picture by a play of sharp tonal contrasts, Turner showed that his concern for the art of the High Renaissance (here the debt seems to be chiefly to Raphael's *Madonna della Sedia*[34]) had persisted into the forties. But in *Rain, Steam and Speed*, a pronounced asymmetricality, a centrifugal emphasis in the bridge and in the locomotive, rushing, as Thackeray saw it, headlong out of the picture, indicate that Turner's debt is to a very different sort of painting; and the handling, too: the feathery scumbling of the central mass of foliage [24], and the way in which,

24 *(left)*. *Rain, Steam and Speed*, detail

25. *Landscape with a Coach*, 1640–41. Rembrandt. Detail of 37.

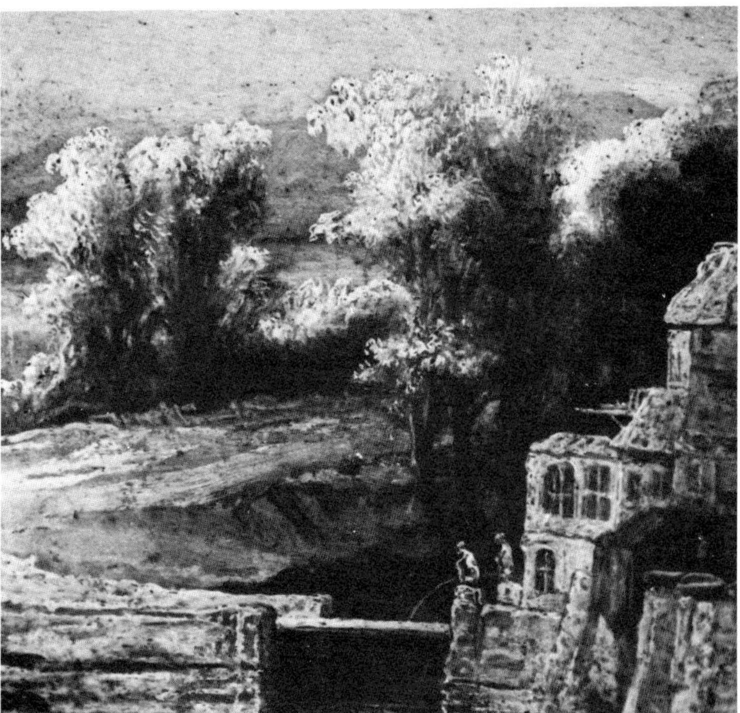

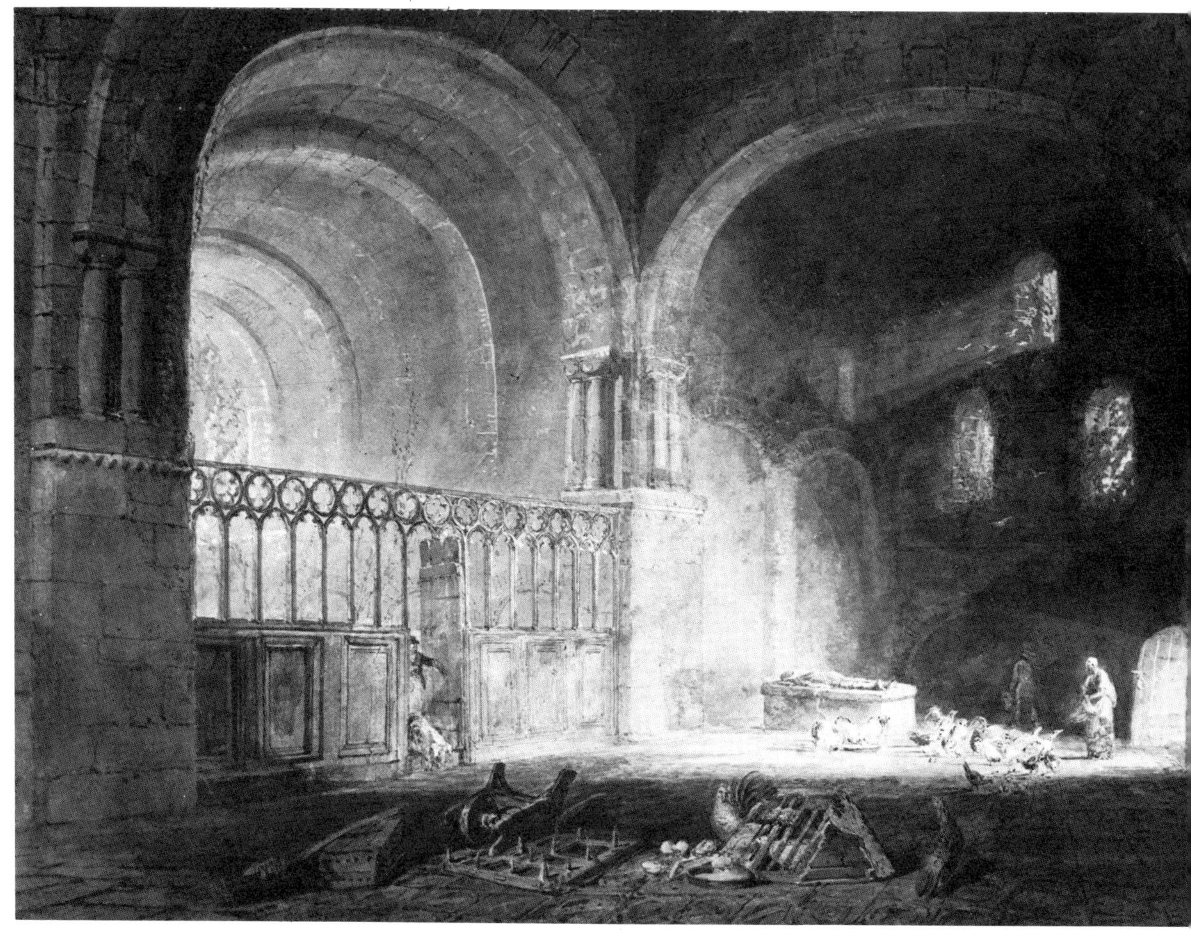

in the bridge, a thin wash of red ochre is overlaid with dense, opaque brushstrokes defining the brickwork, proclaim that this is his last great tribute to Rembrandt [25].

For Turner, Rembrandt shared with Claude the status of a lifelong passion; and, as he is a more comprehensive painter, so he excited in Turner an even more comprehensive response. Turner approached him with a fascination not untinged with the sort of revulsion of a painter brought up within the Neo-classical tradition:

'Rembrandt depended upon his chiaroscuro, his bursts of light and darkness to be *felt*' – ran one of the purpler passages of the

Backgrounds lecture, delivered at the Academy in 1811. – 'He threw a mysterious doubt over the meanest piece of Common; nay more, his forms, if they can be called so, are the most objectionable that could be chosen, namely, the Three Trees and the Mill [41], but over each he has thrown that veil of matchless colour, that lucid interval of Morning dawn and dewy light on which the Eye dwells so completely enthrall'd, and it seeks not for its liberty, but, as it were, thinks it a sacrilege to pierce the mystic shell of colour in search of form.'[35]

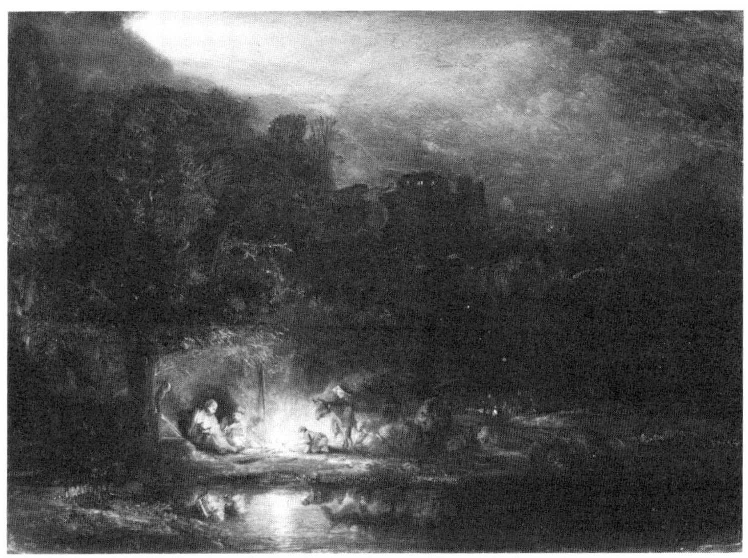

26 *(left). Transept of Ewenny Priory*, 1797. J. M. W. Turner

27. *Rest on the Flight to Egypt*, 1647. Rembrandt

Turner's direct involvement with Rembrandt may indeed predate his involvement with Claude, for he would probably have been familiar by 1794 with a collection of Rembrandt and Rembrandtesque drawings, etchings and at least one painting in the hands of his earliest patron, Dr Thomas Monro.[36] Certainly before the end of the decade he had recognized in Rembrandt a model for his own formation, for the brilliant watercolour of the *Transept of Ewenny Priory* [26], exhibited in 1797 and adjudged by one critic as "equal to the best pictures of Rembrandt",[37] owes both its golden colour and its dense texture to this master. The effect of double-lighting from two directions arose perhaps from Turner's study of the small *Holy Family Resting on the Flight into Egypt* [27], then in the Colt Hoare collection at Stourhead, which Turner almost certainly visited by 1796, and whose lighting he remembered enthusiastically in 1811:

'In no picture have I seen that freshness, that negative quality of shade and colour, that aerial perspective enwrapt in gloom, ever attempted but by the daring hand of Rembrandt in his Holy Family Reposing, a small picture at Stourhead. . . . Rembrandt has intro-

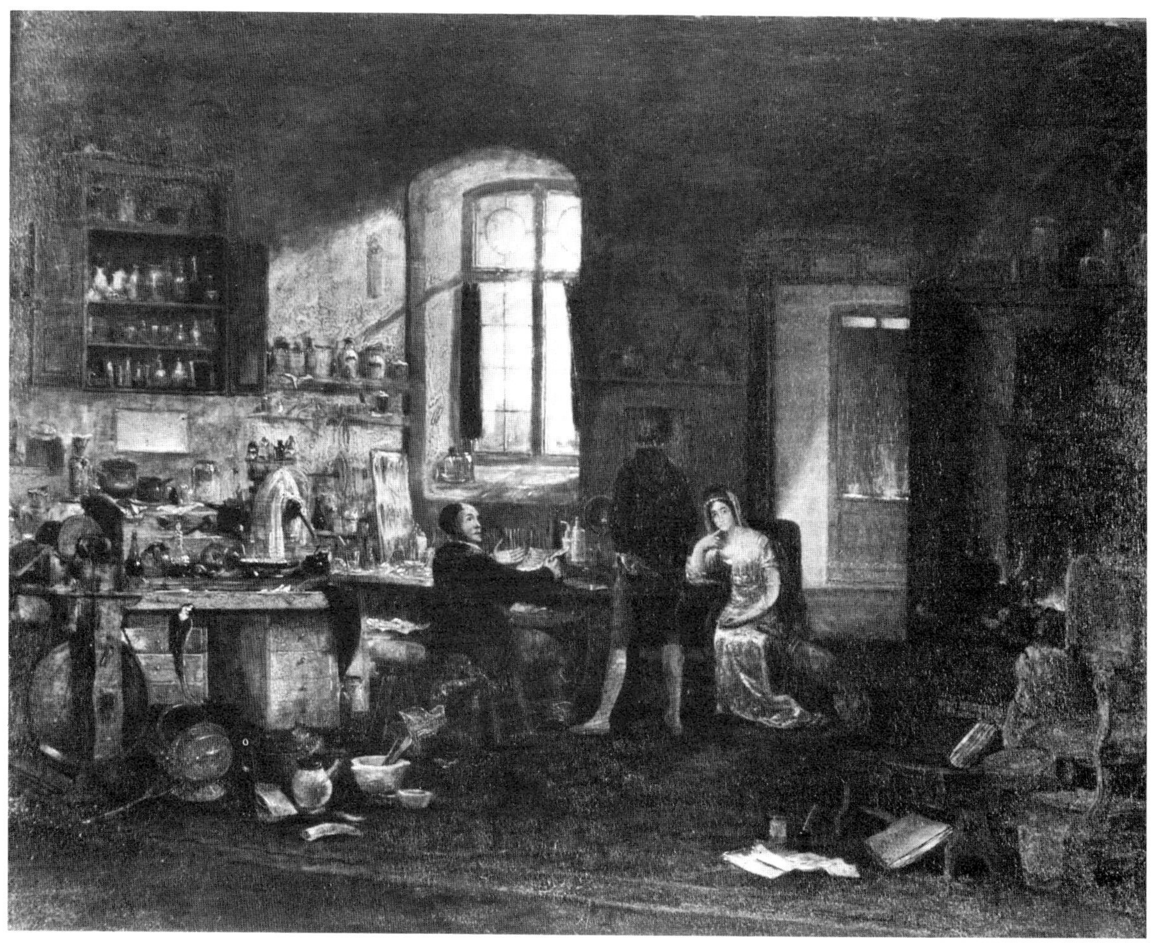

duced two lights, one of the fire and the other from a window, to contrast the grey, glimmering dawn from gloom . . .'[38]

Turner's study of Rembrandt was often more penetrating as well as more sympathetic than that of the connoisseurs and collectors: at least in 1811 he sensed the *subject* of the Stourhead panel, which continued to escape both its owner and its critics.[39] It was indeed an iconographical aspect of Rembrandt which concerned him in his next important Rembrandtesque exercise, *The Unpaid Bill, or the Dentist Reproving his Son's Prodigality* [28], painted in 1808 as a

28 *(left). The Unpaid Bill,* 1808. J. M. W. Turner

29. *The Holy Family.* Rembrandt [?]

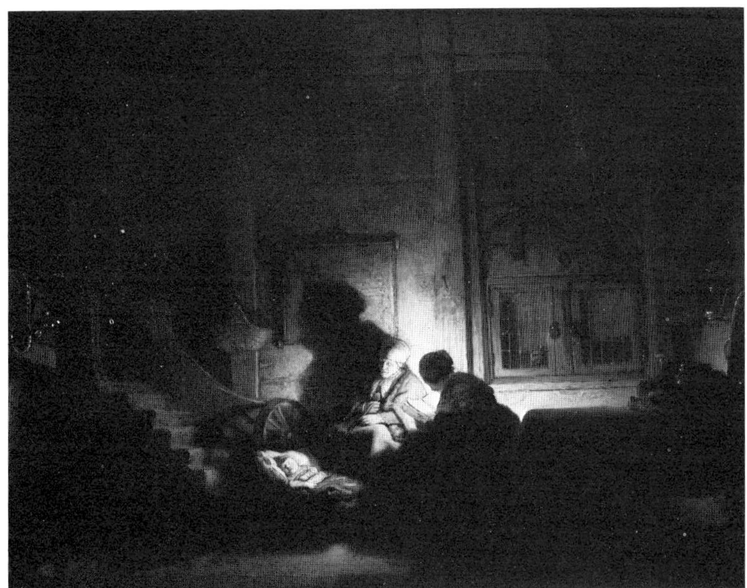

'ridiculous' pendant to Richard Payne Knight's 'sublime' Rembrandt *Holy Family* [29].[40] Rembrandt's painting was universally and simply known as *The Cradle*, and this is the title Turner uses to refer to it; but his precision in matching the infant with the boy, the dozing old man beyond the cradle with his lively and petulant father, and the calm reading Virgin with the anxious mother, suggests that he had felt the subject as well as the solemnity of his model. The spirit of playful commentary persisted well into Turner's

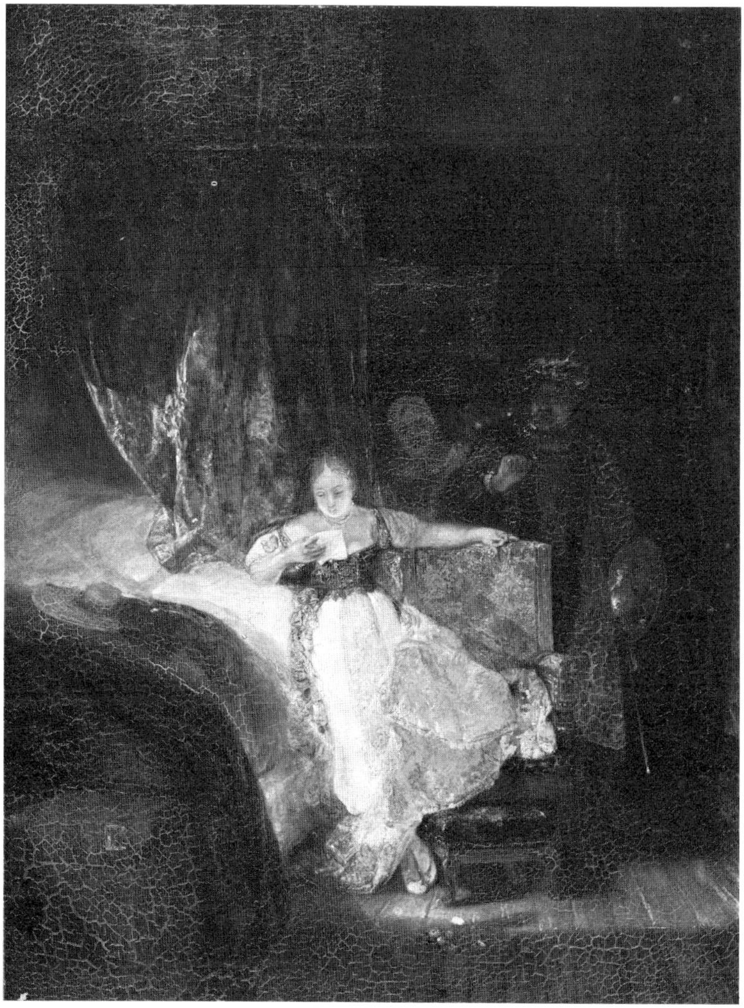

30 *(left). Rembrandt's Daughter*, 1827. J. M. W. Turner

31 *(below). Rembrandt's Mistress*, 1767. J. G. Haid

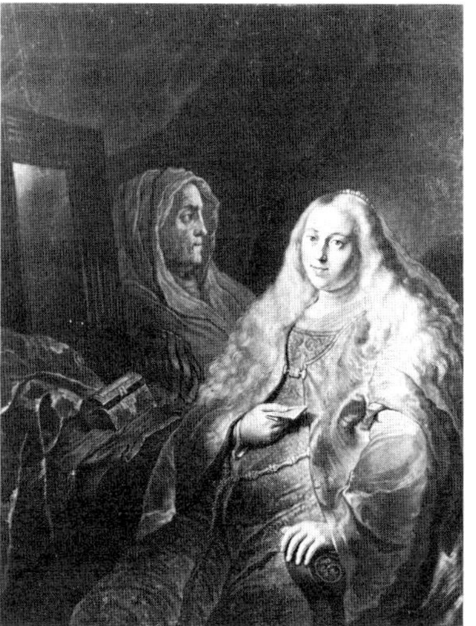

maturity: his *Rembrandt's Daughter* [30], exhibited in 1827, seems to have been conceived within an eighteenth-century interpretation of Rembrandt, characterized, for example, by J. G. Haid's *Rembrandt's Mistress* [31], which had been engraved in 1767 either after a lost Rembrandt painting, or as a pastiche of a number of Rembrandtesque motifs.[41] The common elements of the letter and the background figure suggest that Haid's print may have been the immediate source of Turner's idea, but his picture was also

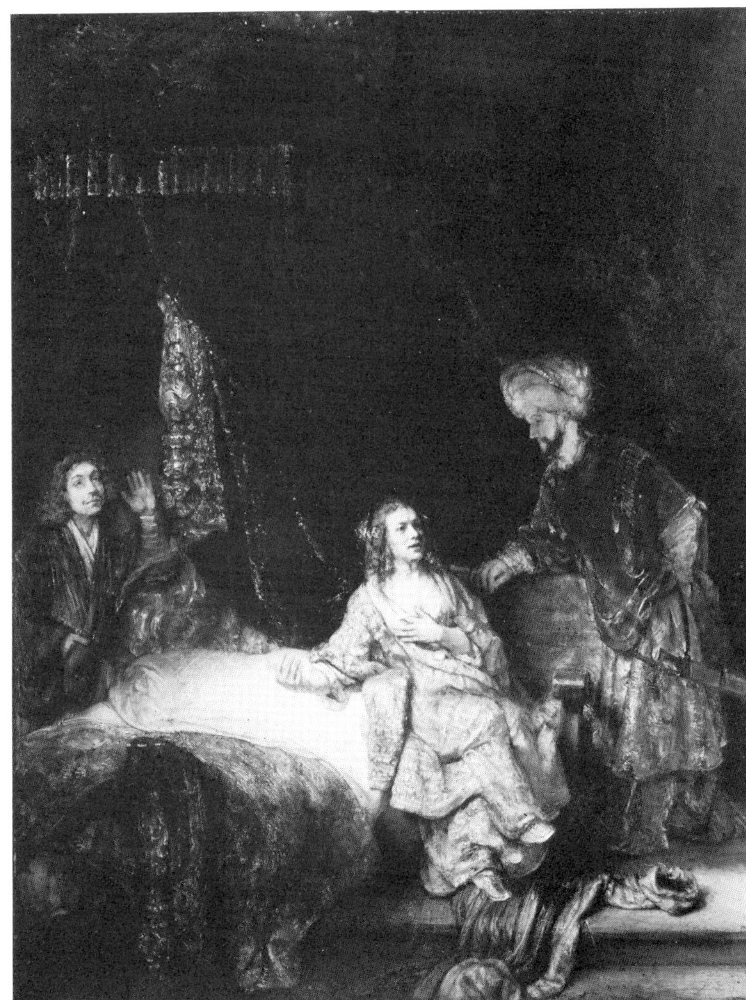

32. *Joseph accused by Potiphar's Wife*, 1655. Rembrandt

recognized as a parody of the Rembrandt *Joseph accused by Potiphar's Wife*, then in the collection of Sir Thomas Lawrence [32].[42] However lame a study of expression, *Rembrandt's Daughter* is hardly a *parody* of Rembrandt's lively comedy of love. Turner had, too, long been responsive to Rembrandt's dramatic pathos, as he showed in many references to the master in his lectures. In a discussion of the expression of sentiment through colour in 1812, he emphasized 'the sobre tone, the darkened yet dignified gleam

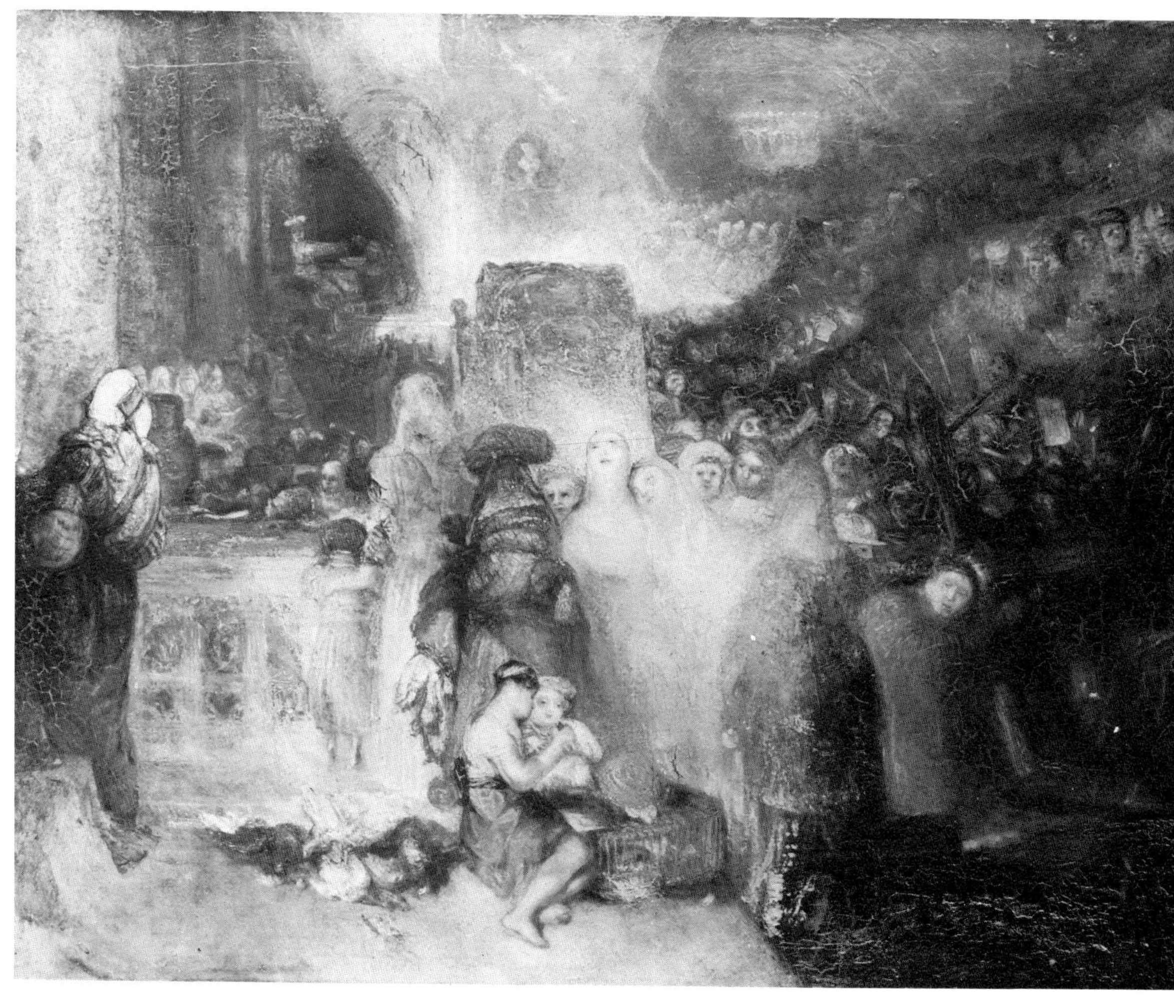

which accompanied every shade of colour in the raising of Lazarus; the half extinguished light on the Resurrection by Rembrandt . . . [which] ask emphatically some designation for that expressive resemblance to which in nature, line by line and feature after feature, and to which poetic colour must assimilate to that sublime exemplar . . .'[43] And in a later lecture he warmed to the similarly expressive power of 'the lurid gloom of the pale gleaming light of Rembrandt, upon the cross and dying Saviour, enwrapped with

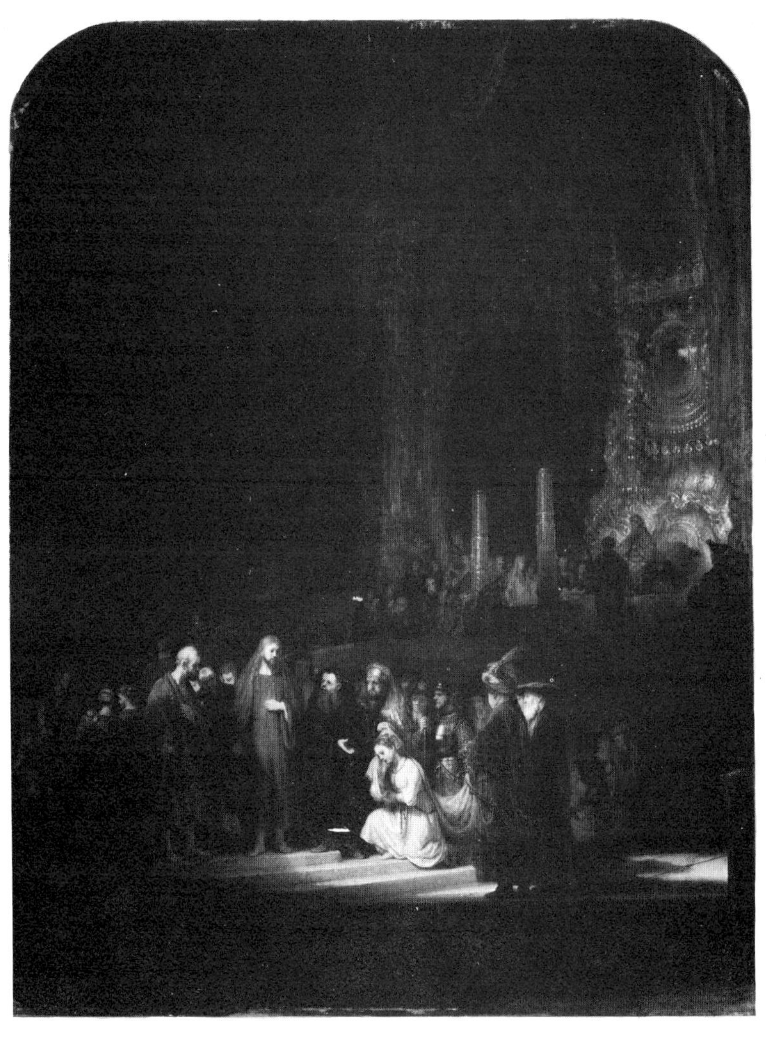

33 *(left)*. *Pilate Washing his Hands*, 1830. J. M. W. Turner

34. *Christ and the Woman taken in Adultery*, 1644. Rembrandt

coloured shade as indescribable in tone as evanescent twilight . . .'[44] That Turner in his maturity was still concerned to rise to the solemnity of Rembrandt's religious painting is clear from *Pilate Washing his Hands* [33], whose setting and mood, as well as the sharp white lighting of the central group may well owe much to Rembrandt's *Christ and the Woman taken in Adultery* [34], which Turner would have known in the collection of J. J. Angerstein, well before it came into the National Gallery in 1824. Turner's conception, in which he all-but submerged his protagonists, Pilate and Christ, in the surging crowd (*cf.* Matthew xxvii, 24), is a perfect inversion of Rembrandt's treatment of his story (John viii, 1–11), where the critics of the adultress melt away into the background. Formally, as well as psychologically and in its narrative, Turner's painting is a parody in the highest sense. According to a contemporary account, *Pilate* was not widely understood among the general public, although the report itself shows that Turner never lacked for enthusiastic critics even at this date:

'When the miscellaneous crowd composing the visitors to the R.A. exhibition first beheld Turner's extraordinary painting of "Pilate washing his Hands", all experienced the influence of its blaze of light, its gorgeous colouring, and magical *chiaroscuro*. But its grandeur of conception, its passion, expression, and pathos, few understood and less appreciated; and the many condemned that which they could not understand, and looked on the noble effort of genius only as a mere mass of unmeaning colour. In our opinion, the grandeur of idea, the power of invention, and the awfully sublime effect on the mind, cannot receive too much praise. The more than chaotic mass, the infuriated multitude that shouted "Let him be crucified!" like an agitated sea undulates before us; we all but hear the Babel-like din of many voices; and, by the distance at which is seen the figure of Pilate, with expanded arms, how admirably is given the idea of space. Like Rembrandt, by the mere power of light and shade, and harmonious colouring, Turner can rouse the sublimest feeling of our mind . . .'[45]

Turner now saw in Rembrandt a model of the highest seriousness; and even at his most personal, in the erotic watercolours that have recently been recognized in a number of sketchbooks of around 1830, he felt close to him, not simply in the fluent, murky chiaroscuro of his forms, but even in the imagery of the shrouded bed, transposed from the joyous Rembrandt etching *Ledekant* (also known as *Le Lit à la Française*) into a gloom of furtive love.[46]

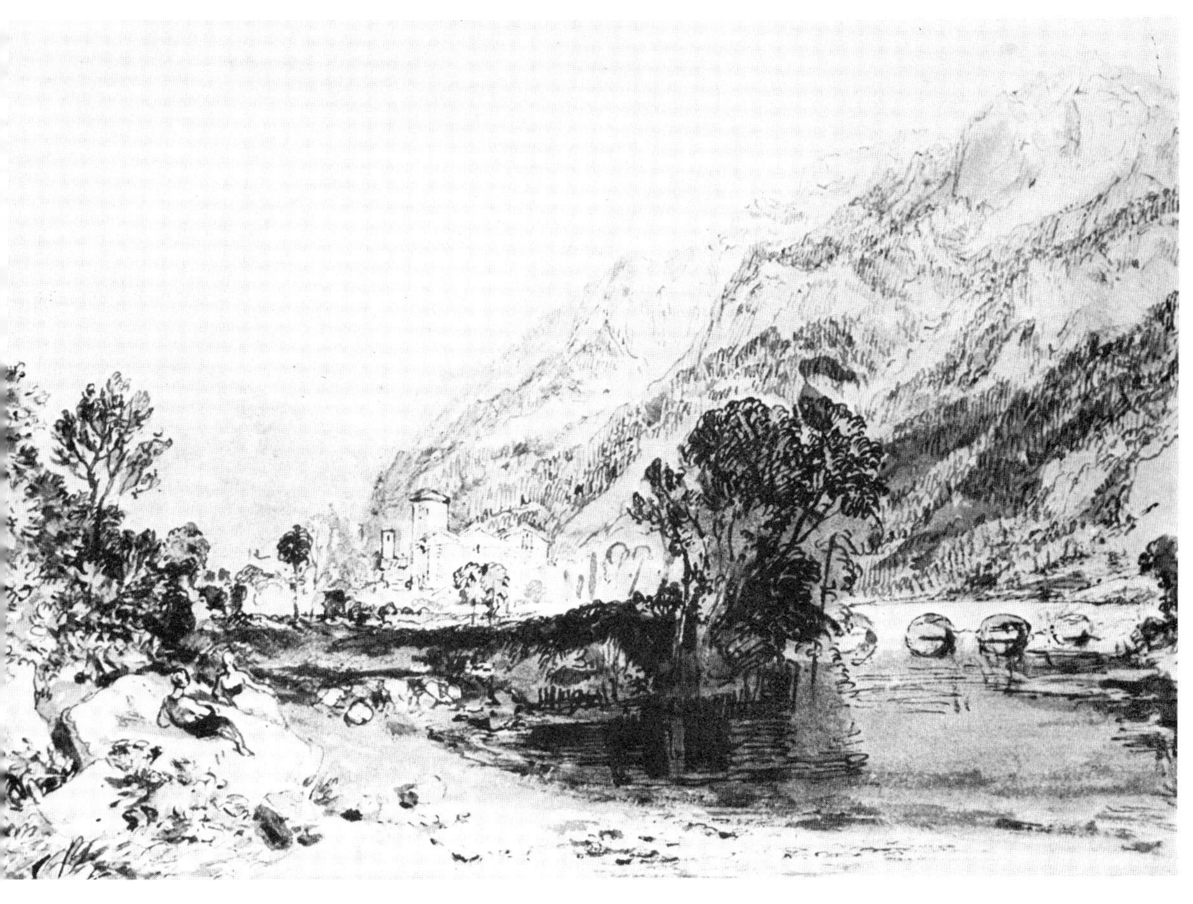

35. *Bonneville, Savoy*, 1816. J. M. W. Turner

But if the public of *Pilate* mistook the sentiment, they did not fail to appreciate the brilliance and technical mastery of this Rembrandtesque essay, and in this they were close to Turner's own feelings, for as his account in the *Backgrounds* lecture suggests, he looked to Rembrandt primarily and most permanently as a model of technique. From the *Ewenny* [26], through the pen and wash drawings of the 1810s [35], which seem sometimes to reflect so precisely a study of Rembrandt's landscape drawings (perhaps those in the Monro collection, or in the British Museum, where the

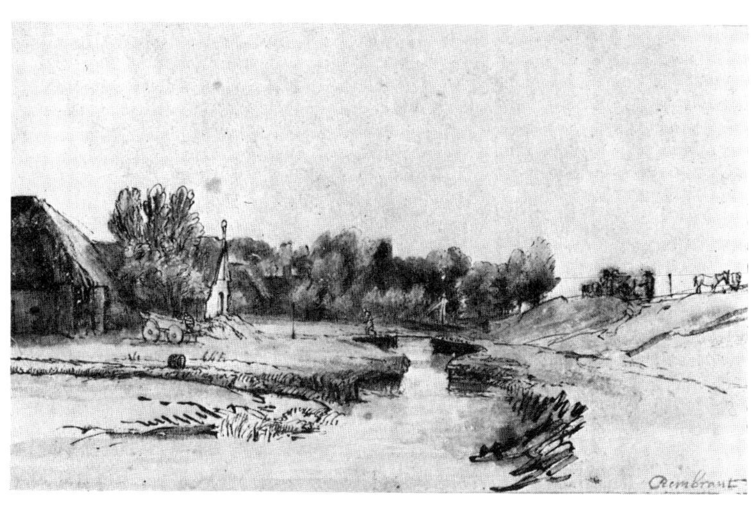

36. *Farm Buildings*, *c*. 1648. Rembrandt

Cracherode Bequest had been available to students since 1799 [36], or, later, at the time of the inception of *Liber Studiorum*, in examples from the collection of Richard Payne Knight) Turner's preoccupation with a Rembrandtesque manner was clearly recurrent until he expanded it into the chromatic virtuosity of *Rembrandt's Daughter* [30], *Pilate* [33] and *Jessica* (Petworth House).[47]

'. . . however much his glowing colour and the matchless magic of his *chiaro scuro* may tend to excite admiration, it is the presence of this soul of art (expression) which constitutes the chief excellence in his works, and must ever claim our unbounded applause. His landscapes . . . owe much of their beauty to the skilful adaptation of this principle. Large portions of his scenes are generally veiled in broad shadows and strong half-tints, relieved partially but vividly with streams of light floating over the surface of the middle ground, or flickering tenderly on some prominent object. These estimable productions of his pencil may rather be styled reminiscences of nature in her grandest forms than exact views . . . breadth and squareness of execution and brilliancy of effect are the main characteristics of his style, and in the attainment of these he scrupled not to use whatever mode or thing might best serve his purpose: sometimes he would apply the stick of his brush to penetrate the dark hues while moist, and develop the ground tint: again the palette knife was found necessary to lay on masses of solid colour as a ground for rich and transparent glazings; and lastly the palm of the hand appears to have been sometimes applied in order to blend the tints together. His colouring combines the richest hues of prismatic brilliancy, so softened and blended by art as to produce the most harmonious effect, and as the pictures by Rubens have with great propriety been compared to clusters of flowers, so those by [him] may, with equal justice, be said to resemble a rich display of costly gems. This perfection could only be attained by preserving the utmost purity and brilliancy in his colours, and by a skilful arrangement of the various hues, both primitive and partial, warm and cold, so united by corresponding tints as to present the most agreeable illusion, always beautifully transparent even in the deepest shadows, clear and delicate in the half-tones and reflexes, and rich and unctuous throughout; ever bountiful with his colour, he spared not to load the high lights with solid masses, which, in some instances, is [*sic*] made to project like the real objects on the canvas, and when viewed from a proper distance produce an astonishing effect.'

Were it not for the references to the breadth of shadows and the 'squareness' of brushwork, we might understand this penetrating account as an analysis of Turner's late procedure; it is however extracted from a contemporary assessment of Rembrandt, and vividly conveys precisely those painterly qualities which must have been so fascinating and so exciting to Turner.[48]

I have dwelt on the history of Turner's experience of Rembrandt in order to demonstrate that his response was almost as much an iconographical as it was a formal one; and if this is so, it becomes possible to suggest a very precise prototype for *Rain, Steam and Speed*, whose handling owes so much to the Dutch master. In

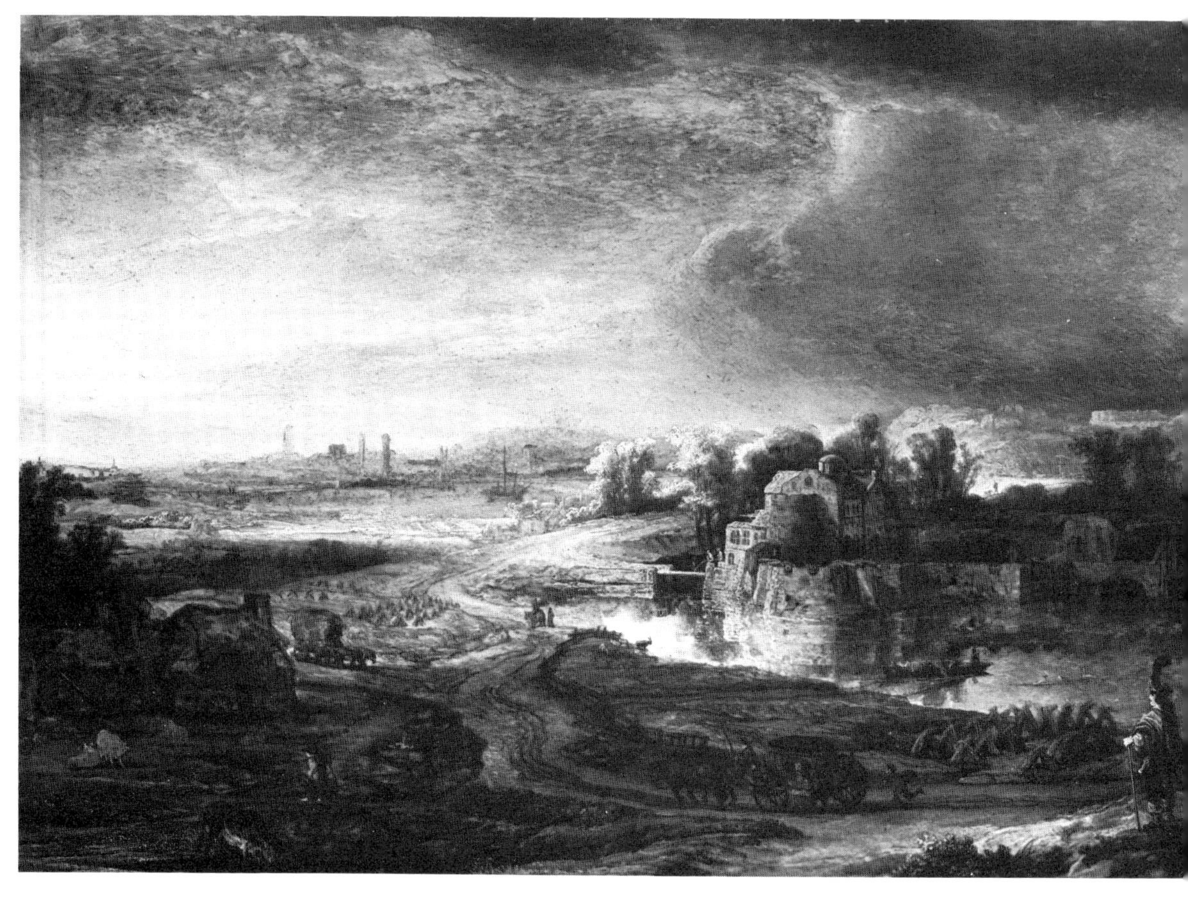

37. *Landscape with a Coach*, 1640–41. Rembrandt

Rembrandt's *Landscape with a Coach* [37], now in the Wallace Collection in London, not only the treatment of the feathery trees [25], but the general, rather frontal arrangement of planes is clearly reminiscent of Turner's painting; and, most tellingly perhaps, it has a little figure running behind the coach [38], which might well have kindled his imagination when he was conceiving his figurative emblem of 'speed'. Turner had had two opportunities of seeing the

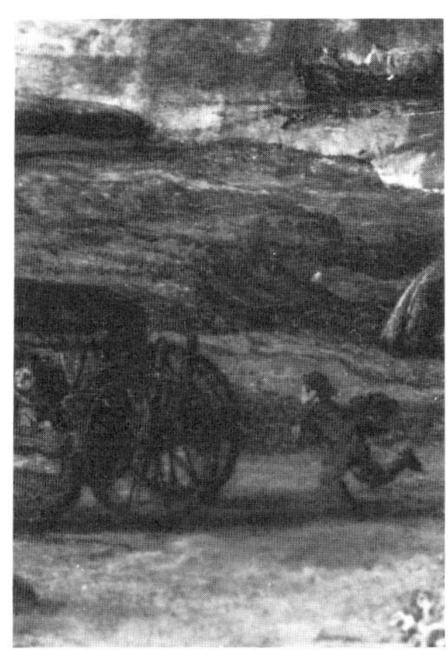

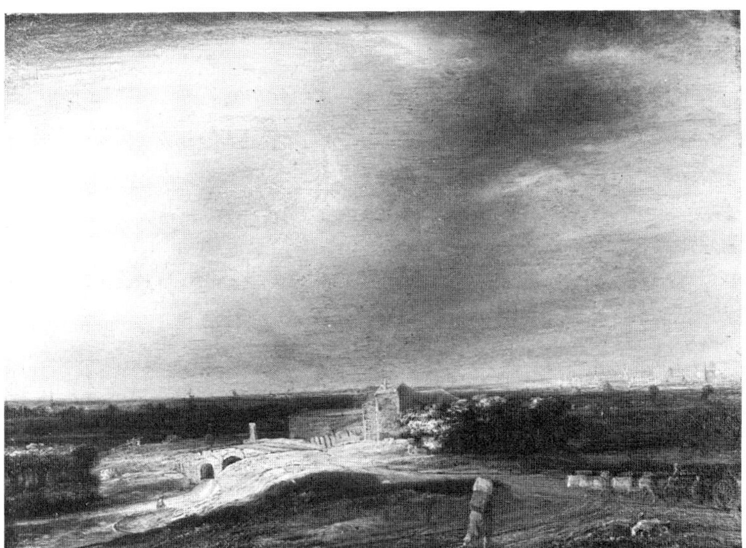

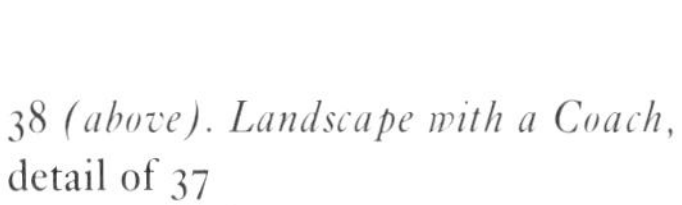

38 *(above). Landscape with a Coach,* detail of 37

39 *(right). Landscape with a Distant Town.* Rembrandt [?]

painting itself: in 1817, when it was exhibited at the European Museum in London[49], and at Christie's sale-room in June 1823, when it passed into the collection of the third Lord Hertford; otherwise he may have been familiar with the engraving by Maillet of 1771. In the year before *Rain, Steam and Speed* was exhibited, another Rembrandt landscape with a similar motif of a bridge, trees, cart and traveller, and an even simpler planar structure, the *Landscape with a Distant Town* [39] was shown at the British Institution; and it too may have helped to crystallize Turner's idea. It would be thoroughly characteristic of his method that the memory-impressions of many years' study came together under the

40. *Grand Junction Canal*, *c.* 1809–10. J. M. W. Turner

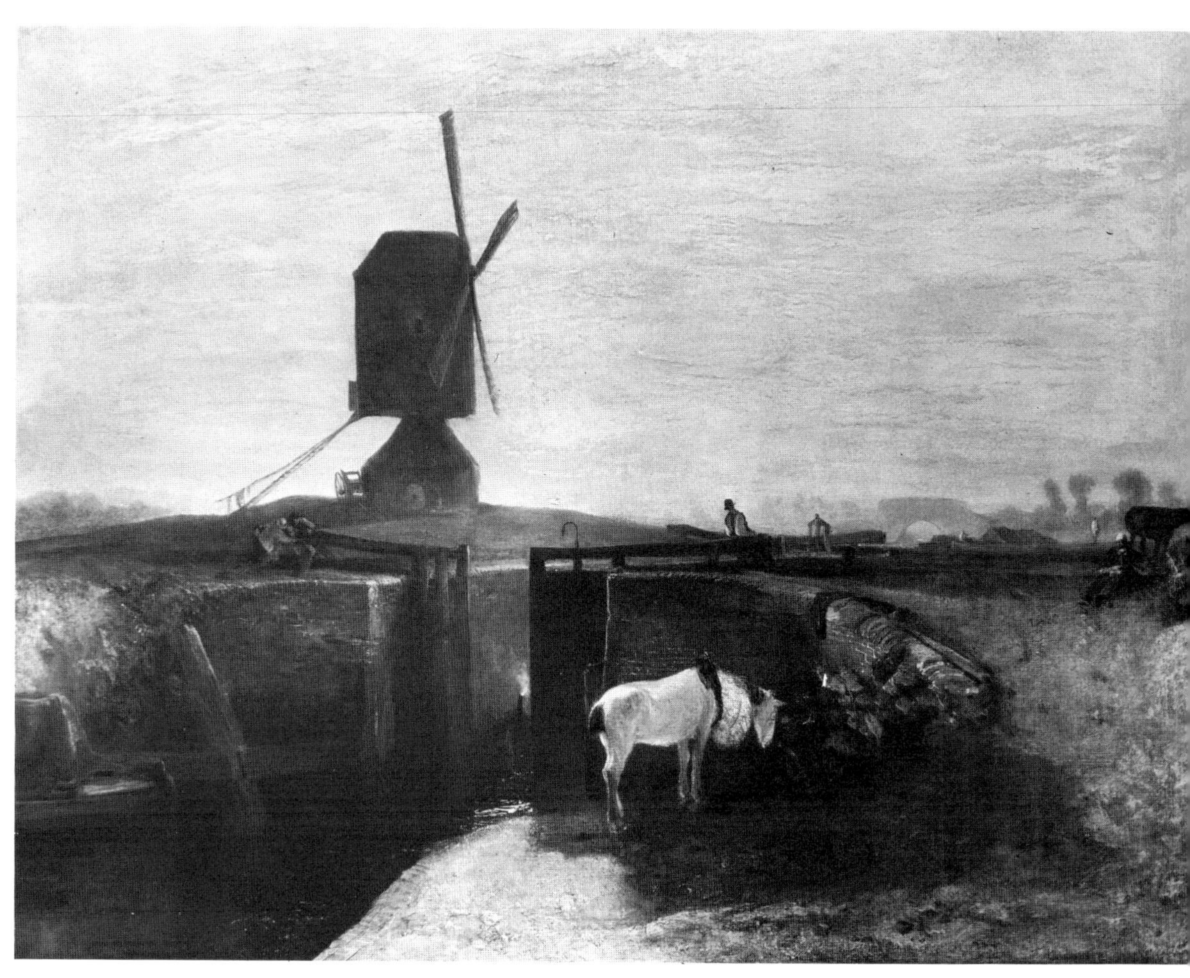

stimulus of an immediate natural experience. If the *Landscape with a Distant Town* set Turner again in pursuit of a Rembrandtesque format, it was surely a recollection of the *Landscape with a Coach* that led him to a more specific, and a more witty motif.

Rain, Steam and Speed was not indeed the first occasion on which Turner had turned to Rembrandt for the embodiment of a modern subject. *The Limekiln at Coalbrookdale* of about 1797[50] shows, with its nocturnal and artificial light, a clear debt to the type of Rembrandt he knew in the *Holy Family Resting* [27]. But the most striking

41. *The Mill.* Rembrandt [?]

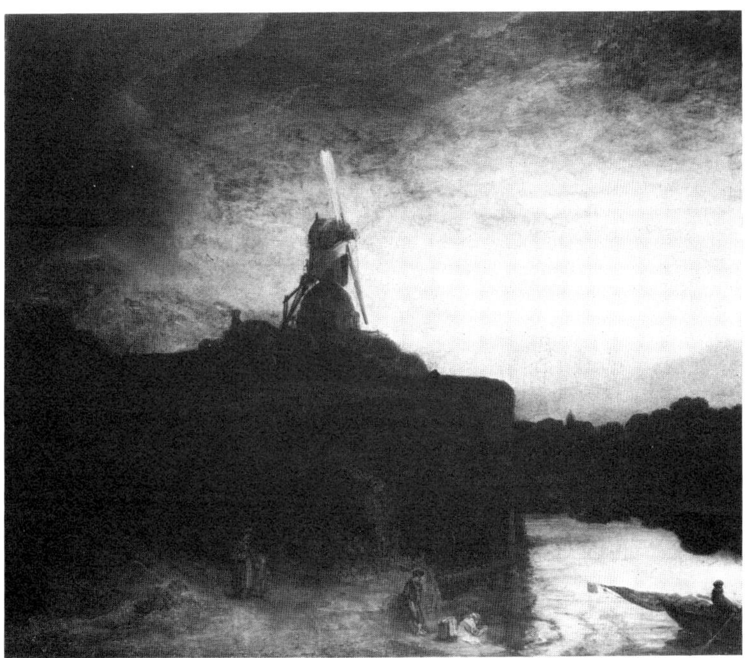

precedent to the railway painting in Turner's early work is in the direct dependence of the *Grand Junction Canal at Southall Mill* [40] on Rembrandt's *Mill* [41]. *The Mill*, although it has now been removed from Rembrandt's *oeuvre* by most critics, was regarded in the Romantic period as the archetype of his monumental landscape art. It had been copied about 1793 by Turner's colleague, Thomas Girtin[51], and it was copied by the President of the Royal

Academy, Benjamin West, when it was shown at the British Institution in 1806 or 1815.[52] It was the first opportunity for study at the 1806 exhibition which gave rise to Turner's *Grand Junction Canal*, which seems to belong to a few years later: on the second occasion, a more purely theoretical interest, generated by the Perspective lectures, stimulated Turner to make a long analysis of the painting in one of his notebooks:

'The Mill has but one light, that is to say upon the Mill, for the sky, altho a greater body of mass, is reduced to black and white [and] yet is not perceptible of receiving [the] ray by any indication of form, but rather a glow of approaching light. But the sails of the mill are touched with the incalculable ray, while all below is lost in inestimable gloom without the value of reflected light, which even the sky demands, and the ray upon the Mill insists upon, while the ½ gleam upon the water admits the reflection of the sky. Evanescent twilight is all reflection, but in Rembrandt it is all darkness and [a] gleam of light reactive of Reflection.'

The Cradle [29], on the other hand, treating the effect of light in an interior, showed Rembrandt to be 'the master of artificial light and shade'; and Turner concluded: 'The art of the Picture therefore is only and properly light and shade.'[53] The *Grand Junction Canal* is a sunset, not a twilight scene, and the palette Turner used is correspondingly far more chromatic than that in *The Mill*, but both pictures are concerned with precisely the same elements of light reflected in water and on or against the mill sails, whose treatment in the Turner as dark against light, offers a variation on the theme of *The Mill*, so to speak, in reverse. In *Rain, Steam and Speed*, too, Turner retained a similar format but altered the lighting of *Landscape with a Coach*, banishing the Rembrandtesque areas of broad shadow and raising the key and colour of the whole picture. Both Turner paintings are concerned with the technology of modern transport, for canals were the engineering triumph of the immediately pre-railway age (the Grand Junction Canal was still under construction when Turner painted his *Mill*). Canals had been celebrated in the 1820s by Constable in his great six-foot canvases, from the *White Horse* of 1819 (New York, Frick Collection), and *View of the Stour* (1822, San Marino, Huntington Library and Art Gallery) to *The Leaping Horse* of 1825 (London, Royal Academy), which treated the canalized section of the Stour lushly, and unobtrusively, with a technique developed from the study of Rubens. But Turner, in both his early canal-scape, and in his railway picture, looked back to Rembrandt for a pictorial language to express the drama of modern times.

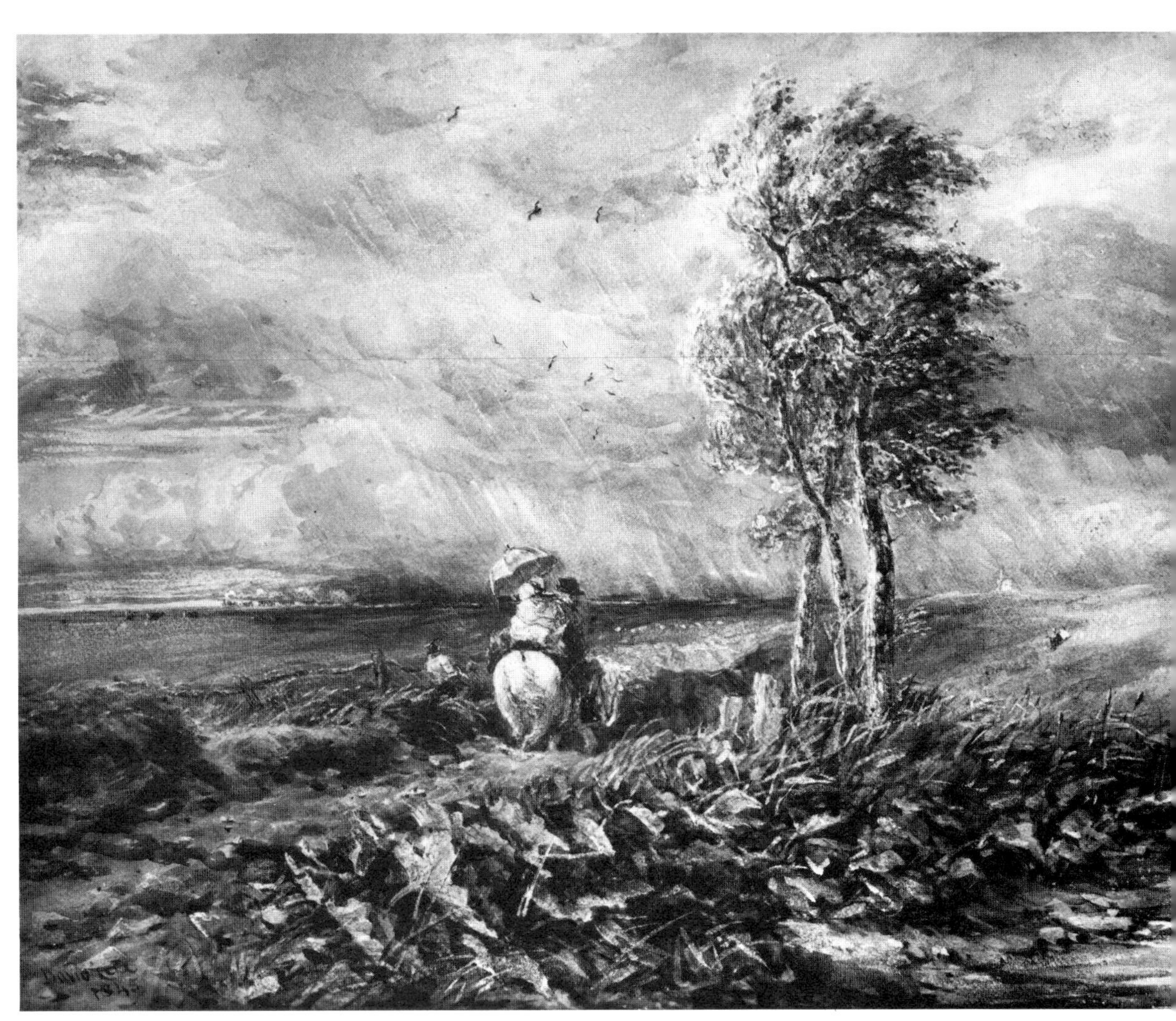

42. *Wind, Rain and Sunshine*, 1845. David Cox

3. The Failure of an Idea

That Turner had chosen to celebrate the Railway Age with an allegory developed from the Baroque, and in a style deriving from a study of Rembrandt, was lost on his followers, who, in any case, seem to have shown little interest in *Rain, Steam and Speed.* A year after its exhibition at the Academy, David Cox, who had probably seen it there, conceived his own version, first in water-colour [42], and then in an oil (now lost), to which he gave the title *Wind, Rain and Sunshine.*[54] The shift of emphasis towards a pure landscape idea is clear from the title; and the insignificant background of the train, even less intrusive than in the earlier illustrations of Carmichael [2], suggests that Cox intended no more than a distant tribute to the last of Turner's paintings he thoroughly admired. Cox returned in the late 1850s to the railway theme in Romantic watercolours like *The Night Train* [43] (a replica, also at

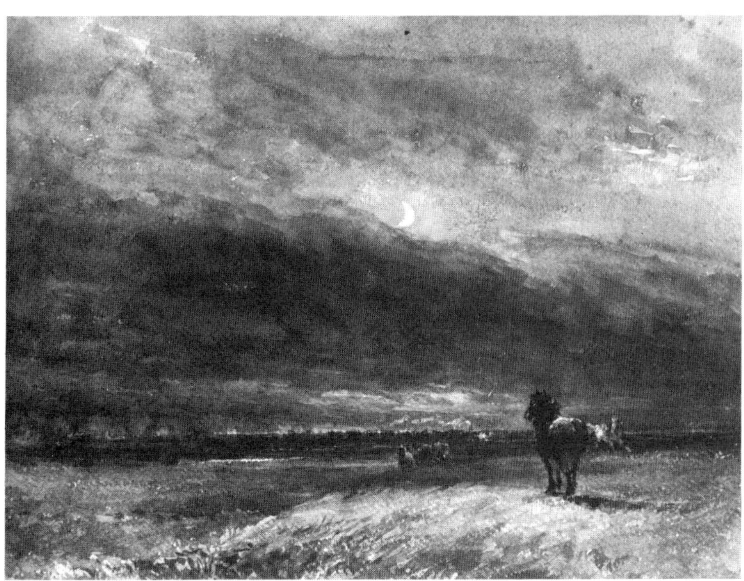

43. *The Night Train, c.* 1857. David Cox

Birmingham, is known as *The Birmingham Express*), but it never held for him more than a passing interest, although he was the only one of Turner's successors on whom *Rain, Steam and Speed* seems to have made any impact at all. His picture seems almost a response to the plea for motifs from technology made by F. G. Stephens in the Pre-Raphaelite Journal *Art and Poetry (The Germ)* in May 1850, although, again, it was never a subject taken up by the Pre-Raphaelite group of painters themselves:

'You point out to others (as if they had no eyes) the sentiment of a flowing river with the moon on it, as an emblem of the after-peace, but you see not this in the long white cloud of steam, the locomotive pours forth under the same moon rushing on; the perfect type of the same, with the presentment of the struggle beforehand. The strong engine is never before you, sighing all night, with the white cloud above the chimney-shaft escaping like the spirits Solomon put his seal upon, in the Arabian Tales . . .'

Some followers, like James Baker Pyne, painted railway illustrations; and in England Turner's picture came to be regarded primarily as a document of realism. Little more than a decade after it was painted its peculiar imagery had faded into the background, perhaps in more senses than one. In 1857, Charles Lock Eastlake, Director of the National Gallery and an old friend of Turner's, wrote:

'In the *Rain, Steam and Speed* the indication of the speed was marked by three puffs of steam, the nearest to the engine being of course the most distinct, the other two gradually less so. The places are still marked by touches of white, but they do not tell. They require to be assisted a little by such means as Mr Bentley [the restorer] may think fit to adopt.

'I mention this because Stanfield and others remarked the three puffs of steam, already left behind the engine as most clearly expressing the idea of speed, and if they are no longer visible it will be supposed that the picture has suffered more than it really has . . .'[55]

No more of the hare and the ploughman in the interpretation of Clarkson Stanfield, who had indeed, perhaps more than any other painter, drained the Turnerian landscape repertory of its poetry, and introduced it into the new era of realism. For Eastlake's correspondent R. N. Wornum, however, as well as for other critics before the advance of photographic reproduction aided time in erasing the memory of Turner's symbolic details, the coursing hare continued to co-exist with the puffs of smoke which had come to be identified with the 'Steam'.[56]

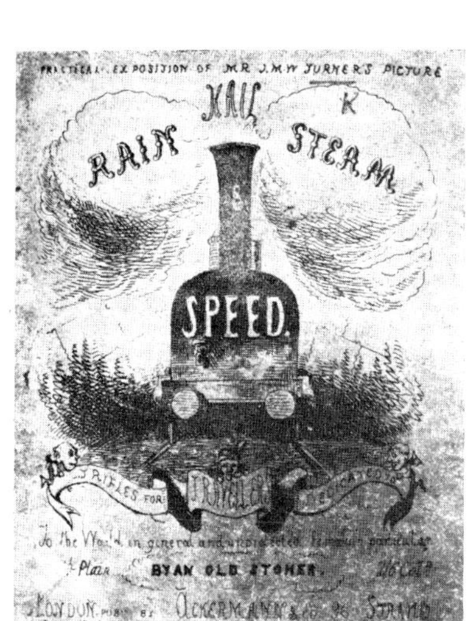

44. Frontispiece, *c.* 1850. G. A. Sala

For the general English public the facetious response evoked by Thackeray continued perhaps to be the norm; and it was perpetuated in the fifties by G. A. Sala's comic pamphlet on the hazards of rail travel, *Practical Exposition of Mr J. M. W. Turner's Picture, Rain, Hail* [*sic*], *Steam & Speed. Trifles for Travellers Dedicated to To* [*sic*] *the World in general and unprotected females in particular, By an Old Stoker* [44], whose satirical drawings have no more to do with the painting than the title under which they were presented. Neither the peculiar qualities of Turner's imagination nor his highly personal style found much echo in English painting after the occasional reminiscences in Cox and Pyne; and the railway subject *per se* passed out of the orbit of landscape into that of Victorian *genre*.

It was, in the event, in France that *Rain, Steam and Speed* had its most significant effect after Turner's death. His younger contemporary, Delacroix, was still happier in the fifties to travel by coach rather than by train: 'If I am not quite so comfortable as in the train', he reflected, echoing Ruskin almost to the letter, 'at least I am travelling, I see things, I am a man; I am neither a trunk nor a parcel' (*Journal*, 12 July 1855). Théophile Gautier's exotic account of Turner's picture in the sixties has already been quoted, but it was for very different reasons that the painting was looked upon with fascination in the last quarter of the century by a group of landscape painters who had initiated the Impressionist movement. On this movement itself it seems to have had little effect. It must certainly have been seen by Claude Monet and Camille Pissarro during their visit to London from 1870–71, but in the railway pictures they produced on or immediately after this trip, there is barely a trace of Turner's influence, unless it be simply in the choice of motif. Pissarro's *Penge Station, Upper Norwood* [45] and Monet's *Railway Bridge at Argenteuil* [46] go back in their quiet objectivity to the pre-Turnerian railway illustrators; and even Monet's *Gare St Lazare* series of 1877 [47, 49], which critics have sometimes associated with *Rain, Steam and Speed*, treats the subject in a searching, dispassionate way more reminiscent of Bourne [48] than

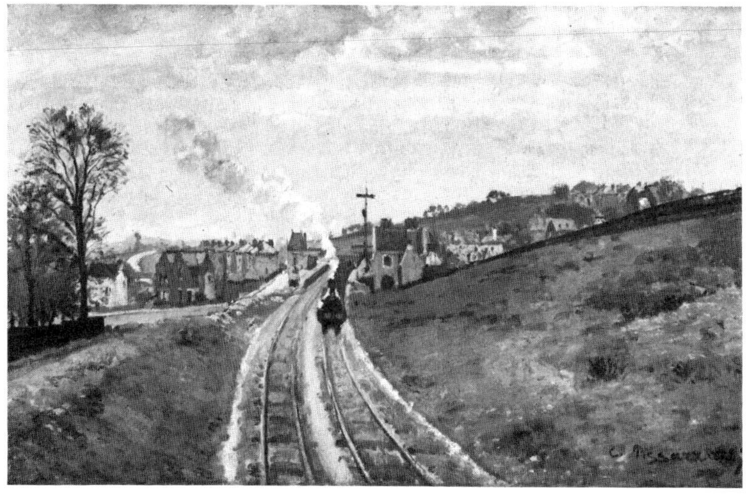

45. *Penge Station, Upper Norwood*, 1871. Camille Pissarro

of Turner. Monet's choice of locomotives resting inside or outside a station rather than rushing through open countryside is itself symptomatic of a very different attitude to the subject; the only exception in the series is a small canvas in an American private collection, of a train leaving the platform, and smoke from one that has passed [49]. Here the treatment of the curls of smoke recalls Turner, although the framework is still one of realism; and it is likely that at this stage, as at the close of his life, Turner was, as Monet told a critic, 'antipathetic to him because of the exuberant romanticism of his fancy.'[57]

46. *Railway Bridge at Argenteuil*, 1875. Claude Monet

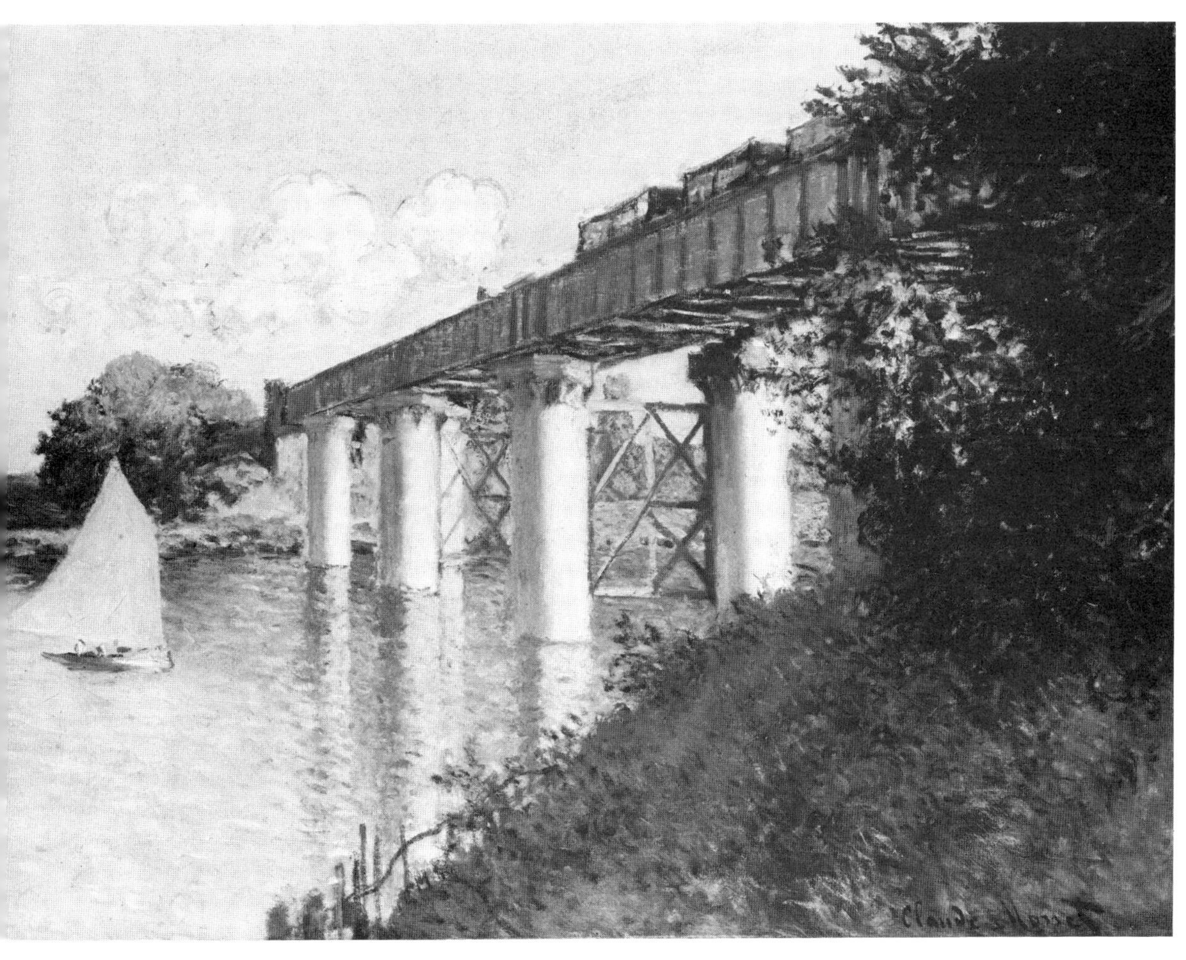

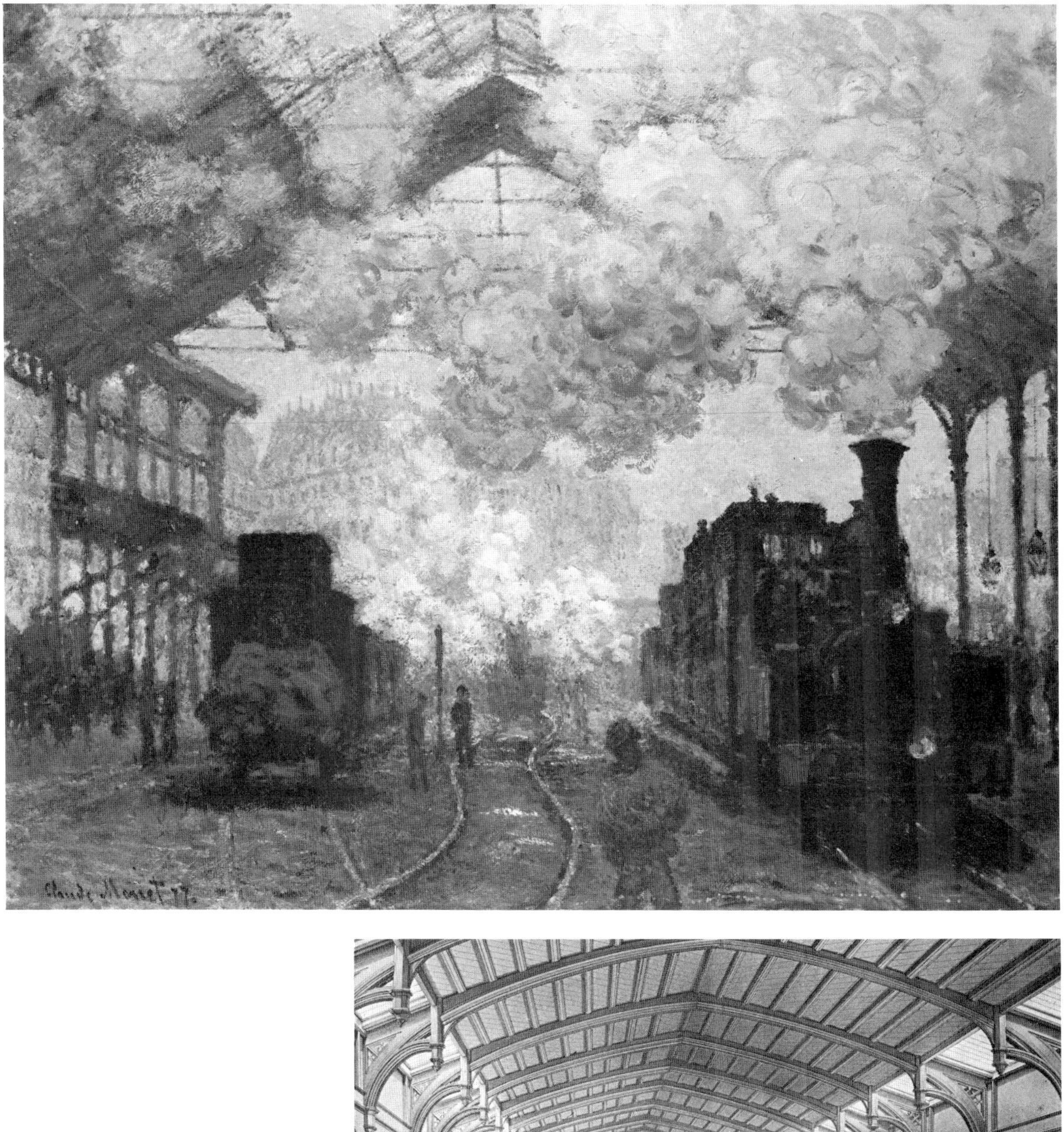

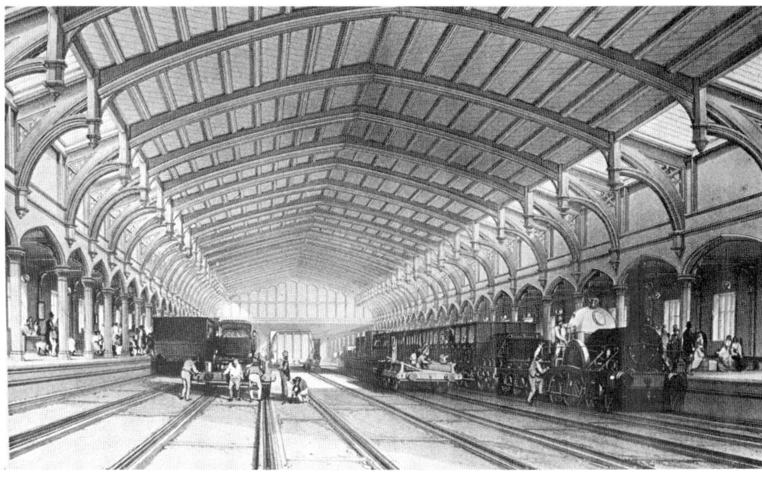

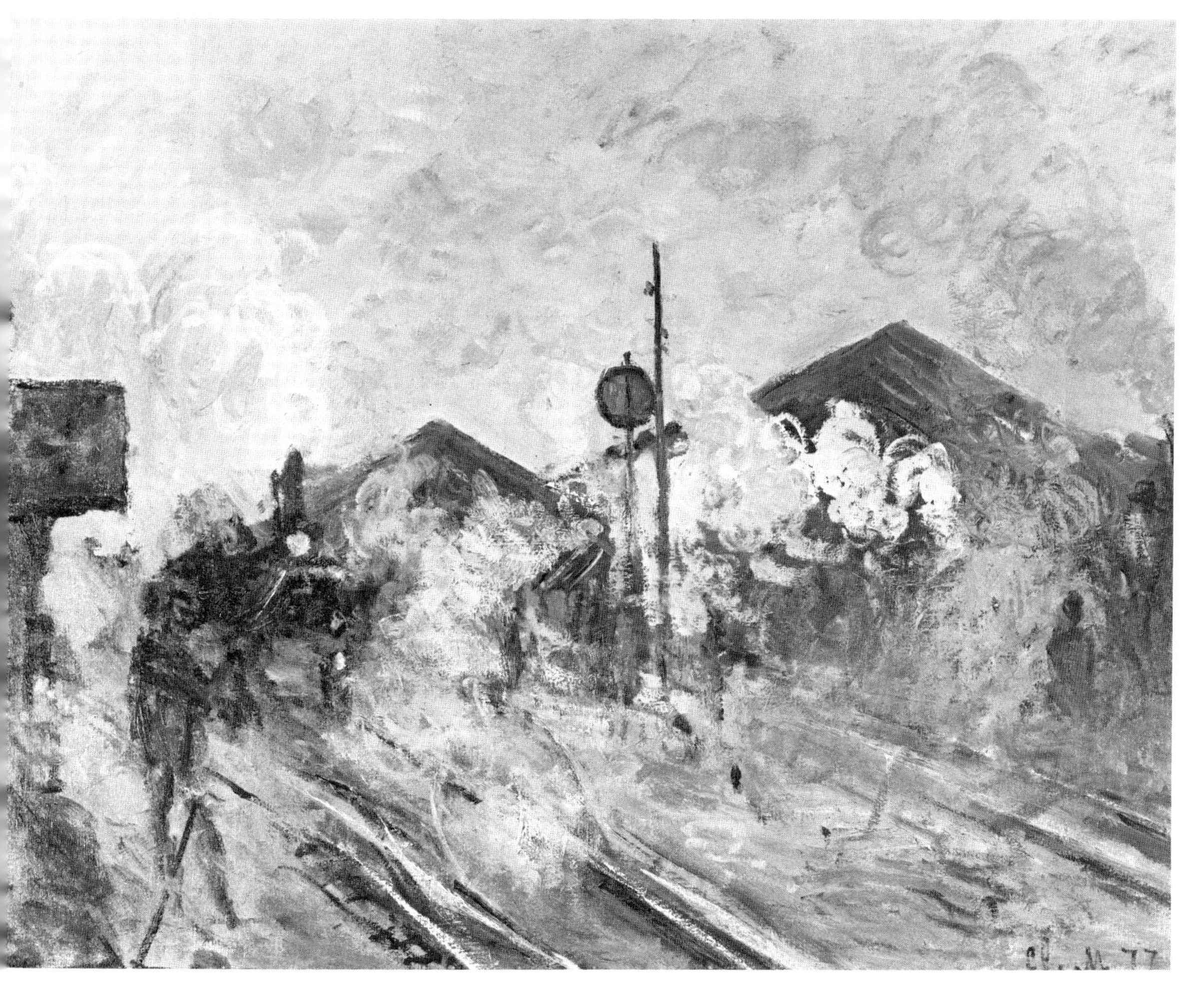

47 *(left above)*. *Gare St Lazare*, 1877. Claude Monet

48 *(opposite)*. *Bristol Station*, 1846. J. C. Bourne

49 *(above)*. *Gare St Lazare*, 1877. Claude Monet

Rain, Steam and Speed had nonetheless left an impression on the minds of both Monet and Pissarro. In the 1880s Pissarro commended the picture especially to the study of his son, Lucien, who was visiting London.[58] The focus was not now on Turner's warmth of imagination, but on the coolness of his pictorial means. Félix Braquemond, an engraver close to the Impressionist circle (his wife was a follower of Monet), referred to the picture in 1885 as 'without special affectation';[59] and in the first sizeable monograph on Turner to be published in France, P. G. Hamerton, although he was at pains to emphasize that the painter had in no sense been a *plein-air* artist, wrote of *Rain, Steam and Speed* prophetically enough for 1889: 'It is interesting to see how Turner has got round the highly unpoetic aspect of a locomotive, rails and a viaduct. The picture answers well to its title: it gives the idea of rain, steam and speed, but the railway is given as little prominence as possible. It is an interesting experiment in the expression of abstract ideas in painting.'[60] The way in which Turner had dissolved his specific imagery in a far more potent imagery of light and colour became the dominant note of French criticism of the picture, and helps to explain how it became so compelling to French landscape painters at the turn of the century. In an important article of 1904 in the *Gazette des Beaux-Arts*, J. Leclercq discussed it together with *Snowstorm: Steamboat off a Harbour's Mouth* [3]: 'In these paintings there is nothing but light and the elements. In front of this train crossing some Thames bridge, leaving behind it the river-bank washed by the rain, and coming on through a damp and translucid atmosphere, we get the idea that Turner's great strength was his complete lack of prejudices, in an age when artists, more than today, were full of them.'[61]

In terms of subject, for Turner, anything went, and in referring to the moderns, Leclercq was probably thinking of Monet, whose latest exhibition of London views was reviewed in the same number of the *Gazette* by Gustave Kahn. Monet's last visits to London had been made in 1899 and 1901, but he had worked on the canvases begun on these trips right through until 1903; his early obsession with painting *sur le motif* had given way to new and more purely painterly preoccupations. 'Whether my cathedrals, my London views, and other canvasses were done from nature or not', he wrote to Durand-Ruel in 1905, 'is nobody's business and is not at all important. . . . The result is everything.'[62] It was an attitude to painting that brought him far closer than before both to the spirit and to the practice of Turner. In 1904 Kahn wrote in his review:

'Claude Monet has noted some rare, perhaps unique moments, so charged with beauty, variety, luxury, that they may seem for a moment to be as unreal as the realm of Queen Mab,[63] and that in front of these fireworks of gold, of rose-pink, of rose-red, of pink tinged with red, of purple, of grass-green, of yellow-green or deep blue-green, one might for a moment dream of believing that these visions are based rather on some principle of polychrome ornament than on an absolute submission to nature. . . . If it is true that Turner fancied hanging certain Turners next to certain Claudes, we may imagine that to put certain Monets beside certain Turners would be to compare two points of arrival, to juxtapose two moments of Impressionism, or rather – since the names of movements are deceptive, and "Impressionism" only means what the word evokes by a train of echoes (involving the influences of Vermeer, Ingres, Delacroix, Corot, Turner, and the novelties of landscape as well as the new study of the street and of the city) – it would mean the juxtaposition of two moments in the history of visual sensibility.'[64]

Kahn's brilliant analysis of Monet in Turnerian terms was not simply an imaginative intuition, for one of the paintings of Waterloo Bridge with which he illustrated his article [50], seems, with its wisp of steam or smoke curling over the parapet, to take up at least one of the elements of *Rain, Steam and Speed*, although there is no specific

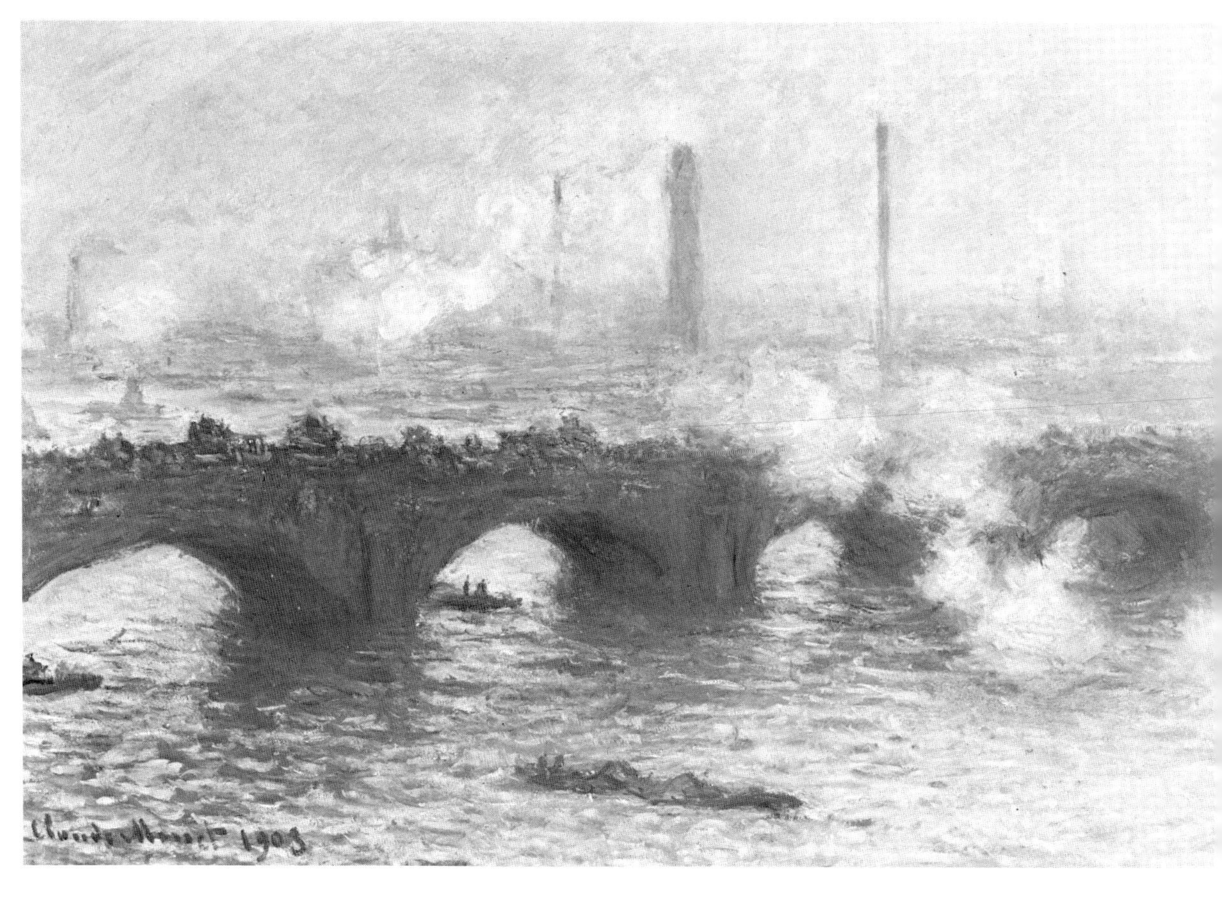

50. *Waterloo Bridge – Grey Day*, 1903. Claude Monet

reference to a railway. Turner's train had been seen by Lucien Pissarro as rushing through fog, and it was, indeed, the London fog, with its own especial materiality, that had particularly excited Monet on his later visits.[65]

In the early nineties, at a time when Monet was developing the bright palette, and the densely hatched and overlaid brushwork of the paintings in series, especially the *Haystacks* and *Rouen Cathedral*, he was also taking *Rain, Steam and Speed*, which he may have seen again on two further visits to London in 1888 and 1891, far more to heart. Echoing the advice of Camille Pissarro, he spoke in September 1892 of Turner to the American painter Theodore Robinson 'with admiration – the railway one – and many of the watercolour studies from nature.'[66] The Post-Impressionist Monet, the Monet of Rouen, of London, of Venice, was able to take up and explore an approach to light and colour that had been explored first in the later works of Turner, and only after he, like Turner, had passed through a phase of obsessive naturalism.

Ever since the 1860s one of the dominant themes in the French criticism of Turner had been his pre-eminence as a painter of light.[67] It was a theme which another Post-Impressionist, Paul Signac, who made an important 'pilgrimage to Turner' in London in 1898, came to regard as central to his own preoccupations. Of a group of paintings in the National Gallery, including *Rain, Steam and Speed*, Signac wrote to a friend, very much in the spirit of Gustave Kahn on Monet: 'These are no longer *pictures*, but aggregations of colours (*polychromies*), quarries of precious stones, *painting* in the most beautiful sense of the word.'[68]

Rain, Steam and Speed was later adduced by Signac in an article on 'The Subject in Painting' as an example of Turner's fantastic choice of a title he could well do without: 'Turner himself seems to have brought some fantasy to bear on the choice of his titles by giving a locomotive, in front of which a maddened hare is scampering away, that of *Rain, Steam and Speed*.'[69] Signac had spotted the image without recognizing its function: the implication was that such a picture might just as well have been called something else. The identity of manner and matter which Turner had sought to achieve pre-eminently in his late work had been lost.

The French reduction of Turner's painting to a poetry of forms and colours has characterized most appreciation of it ever since, and it is surely just. For it is in this that Turner's highly particular imagination emerges from his eighteenth-century Cockney background into the mainstream of the painterly tradition that runs from Leonardo to the twentieth century. *Rain, Steam and Speed* has often been presented within the context of the Industrial Revolution, but as *rapportage* on the one hand and a sort of megalomaniac euphoria on the other were the characteristics of the art of that age, no painting belongs less exclusively to it. In the small canvases of the forties, of which *Rain, Steam and Speed* is one, Turner was showing the Sublime machinists, like John Martin, that size was not a necessary condition of grandeur; and at the same time he was showing the new illustrators like Stanfield (whom he had tried to teach the *painting* of Venetian subjects in 1833) that painters had a duty to painting before they had a duty to their subjects or their age. *Rain, Steam and Speed* was unique in its day, and it remained incapable of producing any fruit in the period of Realism. It is surely as a painting rather than as a document that it will survive as one of the major achievements of Turner's late work.

Appendix:
Wordsworth to the Morning Post

When, late in 1844, proposals for a Kendal and Windermere Railway were mooted, Wordsworth threw himself into the opposition with all his powers: locally, by enlisting the support of the proprietors through whose estates the line would run (Letter 1556); and nationally, through an appeal to Gladstone (Letter 1558), and a series of communications to the London *Morning Post*. The poet had an old connection with a leader-writer on the paper, Johnstone, and he explained to a friend that 'circulation among the Aristocracy is very considerable; all Ladies look at it, and that puts it in the way of the Gentlemen. Besides, the pains, which it takes to support the landed interest against 'Free Trade' and the leagues is the cause of its being a favourite with a great number of the landed Gentry' (Letter 1560).

On 16 October the *Post* published Wordsworth's sonnet 'On the Projected Kendal and Windermere Railway' (*Miscellaneous Sonnets* XLV), with the rather inept editorial comment: 'Perhaps no living man, except the venerable Poet Laureate, would have infused the spirit of poetry into so unromantic a subject as a railroad.' In December Wordsworth returned to the attack with two long letters whose tone and content is extraordinarily close to that later adopted by Ruskin in his chapter of *Modern Painters* (Vol. III, 1856) entitled 'On the Novelty of Landscape'. Ruskin may indeed have known the argument, for the letters were re-published by Wordsworth as a pamphlet at Kendal early in 1845. When this work was reprinted in 1876 (the year of Ruskin's own pamphlet against the Lakes Railway), the editor, Grosart, noted that it was now Ruskin who was maintaining the struggle (*The Prose Works of William Wordsworth*, ed. Grosart, London, 1876, II, pp. 321–41).

In his first letter, of 9 December, Wordsworth examined the claim of the railway promoters that it was their object 'to place the beauties of the Lake District within reach of those who cannot afford to pay for ordinary conveyances'. The poet replied with a remarkable survey of the history of landscape sentiment:

'Elaborate gardens, with topiary works were in high request, even among our remote ancestors, but the relish for choice and picturesque natural *scenery* (a poor and mean word which requires an apology, but will be generally understood) is quite of recent origin. Our earlier travellers – Ray, the naturalist, one of the first men of his age – Bishop Burnett, and others who had crossed the Alps, or lived some time in Switzerland, are silent upon the sublimity and beauty of those regions; and Burnett even uses these words, speaking of the Grisons – "When they have made up estates elsewhere they are glad to leave Italy and the best parts of Germany, and to come and live among those mountains of which the very sight is enough to fill a man with horror". The accomplished Evelyn, giving an account of his journey from Italy through the Alps, dilates upon the terrible, the melancholy, and the uncomfortable; but, till he comes to the fruitful country in the neighbourhood of Geneva, not a syllable of delight or praise. In the Sacra Telluris Theoria of the other Burnett there is a passage – omitted however, in his own English translation of the work – in which he gives utterance to his sensations, when, from a particular spot he beheld a tract of the Alps rising before him on the one hand, and on the other the Mediterranean sea spread beneath him. Nothing can be worthier of the magnificent appearances he describes than his language. But, with the exception of this author, the poet Gray, if I am not mistaken, was the first English traveller whose published writings would belie an assertion that, where precipitous rocks and mountains are mentioned at all, they are spoken of as objects of dislike and fear, and not of admiration. Even Gray himself, describing in his Journal the steps at the entrance to Borrowdale, expresses his terror in the language of Dante:—"Let us not speak of them, but look and pass on." In my youth, I lived some time in the Vale of Keswick, under the roof of a shrewd and sensible woman, who more than once exclaimed in my hearing, "Bless me! folk are always talking about prospects: when I was young, there was never sic a thing neamed". In fact, our ancestors, as everywhere appears, in choosing the site of their houses, looked only at shelter and convenience, especially of water, and often would place a barn or other out-house directly in front of their habitations, however beautiful the landscape which their windows might otherwise have commanded. The first house that was built in the lake district for the sake of the beauty of the country was the work of a Mr English, who had travelled to Italy and chose for his site, some eighty years ago, the great island of Windermere, but it was sold before his building was finished, and he showed how little he was capable of appreciating the character of the situation by setting up a length of high garden-wall, as exclusive as it was ugly, almost close to the house. The nuisance was swept away when the late Mr Curwen became the owner of this favoured spot. Mr English was followed by Mr Pocklington, a native of Nottinghamshire, who played strange pranks by his buildings and plantations upon Vicar's Island, in Derwentwater, which his admiration, such as it was, of the country, and probably a wish to be leader in a new fashion, had tempted him to purchase. But what has all this to do with the subject? – Why, to show that a vivid perception of romantic scenery is neither inherent in mankind, nor a necessary consequence of even a comprehensive education. It is benignly ordained that green fields, clear blue skies, running streams of pure water, rich groves and woods, orchards, and all the ordinary varieties of rural nature, should find an easy way to the affections of all men, and more or less so from early childhood till the senses are impaired by old age, and the sources of mere earthly enjoyment have in a great measure failed. But a taste beyond this, however desirable it may be that every one should possess it, is not to be implanted at once; it must be gradually developed in nations and individuals. Rocks and mountains, torrential and widespread waters, and all those features of nature which go to the composition of such scenes as this part of England is distinguished for cannot, in their finer relations to the human mind, be comprehended, or even very imperfectly conceived without processes of culture or opportunities of observation in some degree habitual. In the eye of thousands and tens of thousands (and happy for them that it is so) a rich meadow, with fat cattle grazing upon it, or the sight of what they would call a heavy crop of corn, is worth all that the Alps and Pyrenees in their utmost grandeur and beauty could show to them; and notwithstanding the grateful influence, as we have observed, of ordinary nature and the productions of the fields, it is noticeable what trifling conventional prepossessions will, in common minds, not only preclude pleasure from the sight of natural beauty, but will even turn it into an object of disgust. "If I had to do with this garden", said a respectable person, one of my neighbours, "I would sweep away all the black and dirty stuff from that wall." The wall was backed by a bank of earth and was exquisitely decorated with ivy, flowers, moss and ferns, such as grow of themselves in like places; but the mere notion of fitness associated with a trim garden wall prevented, in this instance, all sense of the spontaneous bounty and delicate care of nature. In the midst of a small pleasure-ground, immediately below my house, rises a detached rock, equally remarkable for the beauty of its form, the ancient oaks that grow out of it, and the flowers and shrubs which adorn it. "What a nice place this would be", said a Manchester tradesman, pointing to the rock, "if that ugly lump were out of the way". Men as little advanced in the pleasure which such objects give to others are so far from being rare that they may be said fairly to represent a large majority of mankind. But as a more susceptible taste is undoubtedly a great acquisition, and has been spreading among us for some years, the question is, what means are most likely to be beneficial in extending its operation. And I have no hesitation in saying that the good is not to be obtained by transferring at once uneducated persons in large bodies to particular spots, where the combinations of natural objects are such as would afford the greatest pleasure to those who have been in the habit of observing and studying the peculiar character of such scenes, and how they differ one from another. Instead, therefore, of tempting artisans and labourers, and the humbler classes of shopkeepers, to ramble at a distance, let us rather look with lively sympathy upon persons of that condition, when, upon a holiday, or on the Sunday, after having attended their parish church, they make little excursions with their wives and children among neighbouring fields, whither the whole of the family might stroll, or be conveyed at much less cost than would be required to take a single individual of the number to the shores of Windermere by the cheapest conveyance. It is in some such way as this only that persons who must labour daily with their hands for bread in large towns, or are subject to confinement through the week, can be trained to a profitable intercourse with nature where she is the most distinguished by the majesty and sublimity of her forms.

'But it will be said that the least susceptible of the uneducated might be advanced towards the point which we acknowledge it is desirable that all, were it possible, should attain, by still greater facilities afforded for procuring each a look at lakes, mountains &c., and therefore let each man take what he is capable of receiving. Undoubtedly, *if there be no sufficient* OBJECTION, applying to themselves or others, we should concur with those who speak in this strain. I wish, however, to guard them from overrating, greatly as they do in this instance, the amount of the benefit. [*This paragraph was omitted in the pamphlet.*]

'For further illustration of the subject turn to what we know of a man of extraordinary genius, who was bred to hard labour in agricultural employments, Burns, the poet. When he had become distinguished by the publication of a volume of verses, and was enabled to travel by the profit his poems brought him, he made a tour, in the course of which, as his companion, Dr Adair, tells us, he visited scenes inferior to none in Scotland in beauty, sublimity and romantic interest: and the Doctor having noticed, with other companions, that he seemed little moved, upon one occasion, by the sight of such a scene, says: "I doubt if he had much taste for the picturesque". The personal testimony, however, on this point is conflicting; but when Dr Currie refers to certain local poems as decisive proofs that Burns' fellow-traveller was mistaken, the biographer is surely unfortunate. How vague and tame are the poet's expressions in those few local poems compared with his language when he is describing objects with which his position in life allowed him to be familiar. It appears, both from what his works contain, and from what is not to be found in them, that, sensitive as his mind was to the general powers of nature exhibited in storm and stillness, in light or darkness, and in the various aspects of the seasons, he was little affected by the sight of one spot in preference to another, unless where it derived an interest from history, tradition, or local associations. He lived many years at Nithsdale, where he was in daily sight of Skiddaw, yet he never was tempted to cross the Solway for a better acquaintance with that mountain; and I am persuaded that if he had been induced to ramble among our Lakes, by that time sufficiently celebrated, he would have seldom been more excited than by some ordinary Scottish stream or hill with a tradition attached to it, or which had been the scene of a favourite ballad or love song. If this, then, be truly said of such a man, what ground is there for maintaining that wrong is done to a Blackburn or Manchester operative if we be unwilling to accommodate him with a railway to lessen the fatigue or expence of his journey to Windermere for the space of six or seven miles.'

In the *Post* of 18 December an editorial column of 'Table Talk' took Wordsworth's letter as its chief topic, and added to his examples of sensitive men insensitive to the sublimer aspects of landscape that of Oliver Goldsmith,

'who had an exquisite sense of rural beauty in the familiar forms of hill and dale and meadows, with their hawthorne-scented hedges, [but] does not seem to have dreamt of any such thing as beauty in the Swiss Alps, though he traversed them on foot and had therefore the best opportunities of observing them. . . . He associated no feeling of delight with the awful sublimity of the snow-crowned mountains, or the sweet seclusion of the deep green valleys. He only thought of the barren soil and the severe climate. And that so many of us at the present day have escaped from this insensibility to the more secluded and awful forms of natural beauty we in a great measure owe to Wordsworth and his writings.'

Wordsworth's emphasis on the social implications of railway expansion rested on a clear view of the structure of English society in his time. In a later passage in the first letter (which he suppressed in the pamphlet) he wrote:

'. . . passing to the remoter bearings of the subject, may it not be asked, without incurring censure from the truly enlightened, whether, in the laudable tendency recently and widely manifested to deal more justly with the poor, and to provide for their recreation more carefully and extensively than has hitherto been done, there be not some risk of running into the opposite extreme? Without due care, sound principle may branch into sickly sensibility. The constitution of society must be examined with reflection. As long as inequalities of private property shall exist, there must be *privileges* in recreations and amusements. All cannot equally be enjoyed by all. Does it not indicate infirmity of mind even to describe it? Pleasures are much more equally balanced than a superficial observer would suppose. What may be wanting in one direction is, through the care of Providence, more than supplied in another. Of the well-meaning zealots (the word must not be taken in an offensive sense), against whose opinions and practice I am arguing, there may be some, perhaps, who, in passing through the great squares of London, sigh over the exclusion of people in general, and the poor in particular, from the groves and gardens which the owners of the neighbouring houses keep under lock and key. Leave the aristocracy in unenvied possession of such privacies. Be assured that upon the whole the extremely rich are neither better nor wiser, nor healthier, nor happier, than those who stand far below them in the social scale. So far as we may, let us erect and equalise, but beware of short-sighted humanity, lest by attempting more than is possible, or even desirable, we should prove our infirmity of judgement and frustrate the acquisition of good which might otherwise be obtained.'

The double theme that easier access to the Lakes was both undesirable and unnecessary had a ready appeal, and was taken up by the columnist [?Johnstone] in 'Table Talk' on 18 December.

'. . . experience may tell an observant man that the crowd of travellers to beautiful places are merely the lovers of dissipation, who go because it is the fashion to go, or to gratify their vanity of being as well off as their neighbours who have travelled, or to satiate idle curiosity, or, in short, to divert themselves; so that any other place would answer their purpose as well as that where the beauty of nature may be enjoyed. And by not going to those scenes of natural beauty they leave them in that state of retirement which is necessary to their enjoyment by the *meditative few* who have inherited by nature, or derived from education a taste for the beautiful.'

Wordsworth returned to the same theme in his second letter, of 17 December, which he concluded with another sonnet: 'Proud were ye, Mountains' (*Miscellaneous Sonnets* XLVI). 'We have too much hurrying about in these islands', he closed, 'much for idle pleasure, and more from over activity in the acquisition of wealth.' The contrast with Turner's attitude in *Rain, Steam and Speed* could hardly be more complete.

Notes

1. J. Francis, *A History of the English Railways. Its Social Relations and Revelations*, Newton Abbot, 1851 (Re-issue London, 1967), II, p. 139. For railway history I have also used H. G. Lewin, *Early British Railways*, London, 1925.

2. Francis, op. cit. p. 141.

3. Many of these documentary illustrations in F. D. Klingender, *Art and the Industrial Revolution*, London, 1947 (New ed. with new illustrations, ed. Elton, 1968).

4. A. M. W. Stirling, *The Richmond Papers*, London, 1926, pp. 55–6. This account is far less open to objection than the one given to Ruskin (*Dilecta*, Ch. III, §§ 44–9), although Lady Simon described to Richmond how she boarded the train at Exeter, and the Bristol-Exeter extension of the G.W.R. was not opened until 1 May 1844, only two days before the opening of the Academy Exhibition. According to her account to Ruskin, the occasion was a June *night* in 1843. (Curiously enough, the picture was described in the *Literary Gazette* in 1851 (p. 924) as a night piece, and *The Times* critic of 1844 referred to its 'dark atmosphere' (above, p. 13); and the journey from Bristol to Paddington, which usually took about three and a half to four hours, seems on her reckoning to have taken twice as long.)

5. For the background to this picture, J. Ruskin, *Notes on the Turner Gallery at Marlborough House*, London, 1857, No. 476.

6. The bridge seems to have first been identified by M. Davies: *National Gallery Catalogue: The British School*, 1959, pp. 99–100.

7. G. D. Leslie, *The Inner Life of the Royal Academy*, London, 1914, pp. 144 f.

8. I have discussed Turner's development of this type of allegory in *Colour in Turner: Poetry and Truth*, London, 1969, Ch. 8. West's cycle is reproduced and discussed in full by E. Croft-Murray, 'Decorative Paintings for Lord Burlington and the Royal Academy', *Apollo*, LXXXIX, 1969, p. 16.

9. For the symbolism of this picture, Gage, op. cit. p. 134.

10. E. T. MacDermot, *History of the Great Western Railway*, 2nd ed. revised, Clinker, London, I, 1964, p. 468. *Greyhound* was in service between 1841 and 1866.

11. Francis, op. cit. I, pp. 213, 220 f.

12. J. T. Sheahan, *History and Topography of Buckinghamshire*, London, 1862, cit. N. Pevsner, *The Buildings of England: Buckinghamshire*, Harmondsworth, 1960, p. 267.

13. J. C. Bourne, *The History and Description of the Great Western Railway*, Newton Abbot, 1846 (New ed., London, 1969), p. 36.

14. A. Gilchrist, *Life of William Etty, R.A.*, London, 1855, I, pp. 220 f.

15. On the genesis of *Crossing the Brook*, A. Cornwell-Clyne, 'The Birth of a Masterpiece', *Country Life*, CXVII, 1955, pp. 974 ff.

16. *Railway Times*, VII, 1844, p. 500.

17. MacDermot, op. cit. I, pp. 349 f.

18. The fastest average speed in 1843 was the Northern & Eastern's 36 m.p.h. (MacDermot, op. cit. I, pp. 335–40).

19. Bourne, op. cit. p. 2.

20. Francis, op. cit. I, p. 292.

21. E.g. the *Deluge* pictures of 1843 (Gage, op. cit. p. 186). For Turner's relations with Martin, A. J. Finberg, *The Life of J. M. W. Turner R.A.*, 2nd ed. London, 1961, pp. 294, 376 f.; T. Balston, *John Martin*, London, 1947, pp. 124 f.

22. Balston, op. cit. pp. 205 f. Turner may also have had some personal contact with Great Western developments through John Cooke Bourne, whose godfather was held to be one of Turner's engravers, George Cooke, and whose master was another, John Pye (A. Elton, 'The Piranesi of the Age of Steam', *Country Life Annual*, 1965, p. 38).

23. Francis, op. cit. II, p. 147.

24. J. Ruskin, *Modern Painters*, I, Pt. II, sec. I, ch. vii, 37; II, addenda (sympathy for Wordsworth's view); III, Pt. IV, ch. xvii § 24 ('parcel' passage). For the Lakes pamphlet of 1876, *Works*, ed. Cook & Wedderburn, London, XXXIV, pp. 135 ff.

25. T. Gautier, *Histoire du Romantisme*, 3rd ed. Paris, 1877, p. 371. This sensational, if not Apocalyptic vision, of the railway, reminiscent of the sublimities of John Martin, whose engravings had found a ready welcome in French literary circles (see J. Seznec, *John Martin en France*, London, 1963), was still being retailed as late as 1880 by a writer in the *Magazine of Art* who felt, none the less, that Turner's 'chromatic glamour' had sold the subject somewhat short. (E. Bradbury, 'Pictures in Trains',

Magazine of Art, III, 1880, pp. 107–11. I owe the reference to the kindness of John House.)

26. C. Monkhouse, *The Turner Gallery*, London, 1878, III, n.p.

27. Francis, op. cit. I, p. 292.

28. For a recent survey of the Industrial Picturesque, E. Moir, *The Discovery of Britain*, London, *1540–1840*, 1964, Ch. 8.

29. Turner to James Holworthy, 7 January 1826, British Museum, Add. MSS. 50118, f. 67, published C. Monkhouse, *Magazine of Art*, 1900, p. 403.

30. Turner to C. L. Eastlake, 16 February [?] 1829, Maggs Bros *Catalogue of Autographs* 238, 1914, No. 2065 (with the mistaken date 16 November 1829). The punctuation is mine.

31. For Turner's account of Staffa, Finberg, op. cit. pp. 332 f; for *Snowstorm*, above, note 5.

32. Turner to Cobb, 7 October 1840, British Museum Add. MSS 50119, f. 119, published by Finberg, op. cit. p. 381.

33. W. Etty to Gillot, 7 September 1846 (*Connoisseur Year Book*, 1958, p. 75). A locomotive *Comet* ran on the G.W.R. from 1840–71.

34. Raphael's tondo had played a leading role in Turner's programme-picture, *Rome from the Vatican* of 1820 (Gage, op. cit. p. 122), and Turner was experimenting at the time of *Snowstorm* especially with circular compositions (*Glaucus & Scylla* and the *Flight into Egypt* of 1841; the *Deluge* pair of 1843). I have discussed Turner's concern with abstract compositional or colour ideas from the Old Masters in *Colour in Turner*, pp. 64 ff.

35. J. Ziff, '"Backgrounds, an Introduction of Architecture and Landscape", A Lecture by J. M. W. Turner', *Journal of the Warburg and Courtauld Institutes*, XXVI, 1963, p. 145. It is noticeable that Turner's critique is fully in line with that which Winckelmann had inserted, as Devil's Advocate, into his anonymous attack on his own *Gedanken* of 1755: 'Through the magic of poetic colours [Rembrandt's] errors vanish, and he who can read him with the same fire with which he created his poetry will be rapt by the divine harmony into such a state of enchantment that he has no time to think of anything that jars.' (*Sendschreiben über die Gedanken von der Nachahmung der griechischen Werke in der Malerey und Bildhauerkunst*, Dresden, Leipzig, 1756, re-issue in J. J. Winckelmann, *Kunsttheoretische Schriften*, Baden-Baden, Strasbourg 1962 I, p. 75. The version quoted by C. Justi, *Winckelmann und seine Zeitgenossen*, 2nd ed. Leipzig, 1898, I, p. 397, specifies Rembrandt where

the 1756 edition names no painter in particular.) Winckelmann's English translator, Henry Fuseli, held very similar views, and may have passed them on to Turner: (for his and other English Romantic assessments of Rembrandt see *Burlington Magazine*, CVII, 1965, pp. 80 f.).

36. In 1804 (Christie, 23 March, Lot 22) Monro sold twelve Rembrandt prints. At his sale in 1833 (Christie, 26 June) were the following drawings attributed to Rembrandt; Lot 76, *Taking down from the Cross*; Lot 77, *Christ disputing with the Doctors*, and *Flight into Egypt*; Lot 79, *Arrival of Queen of Sheba*. At the sale on 27 June, Lot 36 was *Tobit and the Angel* and Lot 38, *Landscape with Buildings and Trees*. None of these lots can be identified with known Rembrandt drawings. At the 1 July Sale, Lot 38 was *Imitations of Rembrandt's Landscapes*, and Lot 179 the only Rembrandt painting in Monro's collection: *Condemnation of Haman: Esther seated in a rich dress of white satin, under a canopy: Ahaseurus is standing to the right; brilliantly coloured, from the Colonna Palace*. The provenance may be a confusion with C. A. de Calonne, at whose sale in London in 1795 a Rembrandt of this subject was sold for 55 guineas (W. Buchanan, *Memoirs of Painting*, London, 1824, vol. 1 p. 246), and the description suggests perhaps a variant of the early painting now in Raleigh, North Carolina Museum of Art (Bredius/Gerson, *Rembrandt*, London, 1969, No. 631 as Lievens).

37. Finberg, op. cit. p. 43. 38. Ziff, op. cit. p. 141.

39. Colt Hoare regarded it as 'A Moonlight, in which some gypsies are reposing by a fire-side' (*The History of Modern Wiltshire*, London, 1822, I, p. 77). The connoisseur J. Smith listed the picture simply as *Landscape at Night*. (*A Catalogue Raisonné of the Works of the Most Eminent Dutch . . . Painters*, London, vol. VII, 1836, No. 603).

40. For the circumstances of this commission, 'Turner and the Picturesque, II', *Burlington Magazine*, CVII, 1965, pp. 76, 79. The *Holy Family* is now generally given to a Rembrandt follower (Bredius/Gerson, op. cit. No. 568).

41. Haid's design is related to the Prado *Sophonisba receiving the poisoned Cup* (Bredius/Gerson, op. cit. No. 468); and to the Leningrad *Bathsheba at her Toilet* (Bredius/Gerson, op. cit. No. 506), neither of which, however, seems to have been engraved in the eighteenth century. It also perhaps owes something to the etching *The Great Jewish Bride* (Münz No. 90).

42. British Museum Print Room, *The Whitley Papers* s.v. 'Turner', although the reference Whitley gives (*New Monthly Magazine* vol. 21,

1827, p. 379) suggests simply that *Rembrandt's Daughter* may be 'a joke upon Rembrandt and upon the taste of his admirers', without specifying Lawrence's picture.

43. Gage, op. cit. pp. 200 ff. I have hitherto associated the reference to *Lazarus* with the painting by Guercino in the Louvre, which was copied by Turner in 1802, but he may well be thinking of Rembrandt's etching, *The Raising of Lazarus* (Münz No. 192), and, similarly, the *Resurrection* may refer to the Hess engraving (*c.* 1780) after the Munich picture (Hofstede de Grote No. 141).

44. Lecture V, 1818: Gage, op. cit. p. 208. I have there linked this reference with the small painting of the *Deposition*, then in the Beaumont collection and now in the National Gallery (No. 43 Bredius/Gerson, op. cit. No. 565); but it seems more likely that Turner is describing the large etching of *The Three Crosses* (Münz No. 223).

45. A critic 'of about that period', cit. J. Dafforne, *The Works of J. M. W. Turner R.A.*, London, 1883, pp. 67–8.

46. Münz No. 269; some of Turner's watercolours in L. Gowing, *Turner: Imagination and Reality*, New York, 1966, p. 25. There are, however, similar scenes among the Petworth gouaches (B.M.T.B. CCXLIV), which also date from about 1830.

47. Colour reproductions of *Rembrandt's Daughter* in *The Studio*, 66, 1915–16, facing p. 278, and of *Pilate*, in Sir J. Rothenstein and M. Butlin, *Turner*, London, 1964, pl. XI. Of the *Jessica*, Wordsworth, who saw the picture at the Academy in 1830, asked the journalist William Jerdan 'Did you ever see anything like that? . . . It looks to me as if the painter had indulged in raw liver when he was very unwell.' Jerdan added, 'it was a perfectly applicable and just critique. The picture was yellow ochre, with dabs of dirty clotted brownish-red upon it; and Jessica . . . was leaning out of a casement quite in keeping with the other colours' (W. Jerdan, *An Autobiography*, London, IV, 1853, p. 240). If *Jessica* refers to Rembrandt's Chicago *Young Woman at a Door* (Bredius/Gerson, op. cit. No. 367), which Turner may have seen at the British Institution in 1818, or in the London Saleroom in 1829, its high colour had a very specific connotation, for in the caption in the R.A. catalogue, Shylock asks Jessica to shut out the light that causes it by closing the window.

48. J. Smith, *Catalogue Raisonné*, vol. VII, pp. XXXIV–XXXVI.

49. I owe this information to the kindness of Mr F. J. B. Watson.

50. The painting is illustrated in Klingender, op. cit. p. 127.

51. A. P. Oppé in *Burlington Magazine*, XCVII, 1955, p. 395.

52. For the 1806 exhibition, W. T. Whitley, *Art in England 1800–1820*, 1928, p. 111. A copy attributed to John Crome is in the Norwich Castle Museum and a variant by James Ward, signed and dated 1806, was sold by Sotheby, 9 May 1951. For a characteristic analysis of Rembrandt's technique (in *Christ and Woman taken in Adultery* [34]) by West, J. Farington, *Diary*, 10 June 1807 ed. Grieg, London, IV, 1924, p. 150.

53. Gage, op. cit. pp. 198 ff. The notebook (British Museum Turner Bequest CII) was in use in 1808, and I have hitherto assumed that the note belongs to this date; but the exhibition of Rembrandt's *Mill* and *Cradle* at the British Institution in 1815, together with another picture by Van Dyck, mentioned by Turner in the same passage as to be seen there, makes it very probable that the note was a later addition.

54. In a letter to his son of 7 January 1846, Cox described this picture, a canvas about 26 x 18 ins (N. Solly, *Memoir of the Life of David Cox*, London, 1873, p. 139).

55. Eastlake to Wornum, 15 June 1857 (London, National Gallery Archive). It is notable that the most important railway picture close in time to Turner's – Adolph von Menzel's *Die Berlin-Potsdamer Bahn* [51], which goes back to a drawing of 1845 – depends in style on a realist

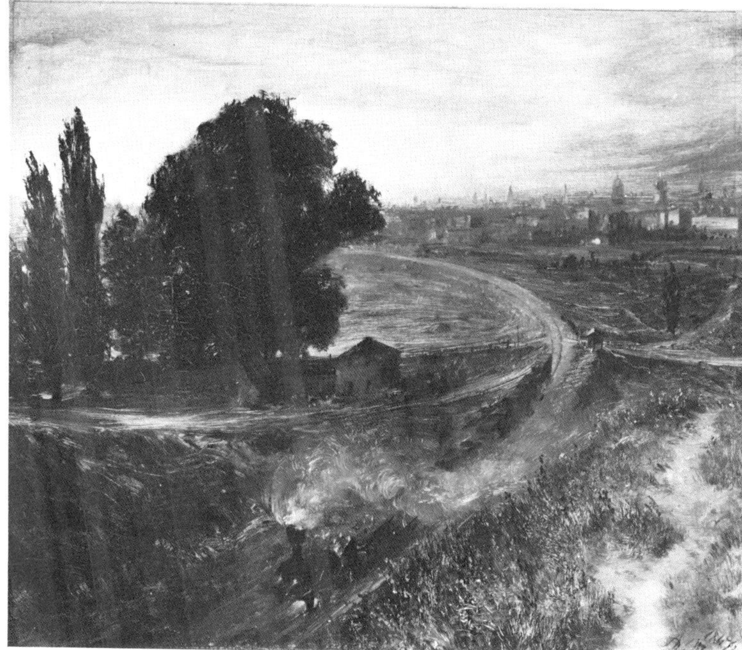

51. *Die Berlin–Potsdamer Bahn*, 1847. Adolph von Menzel

tradition in German landscape, reinforced perhaps by contact with the work of Constable, examples of which were shown in Berlin in 1839.

56. R. N. Wornum, *The Turner Gallery*, London, 1875, p. 90; cf. C. Monkhouse, *The Turner Gallery*, loc. cit.; W. Thornbury, *The Life and Correspondence of J. M. W. Turner*, 2nd ed. London, 1904, p. 92. The engraving by R. Brandard (1859) used in both editions of *The Turner Gallery* shows the hare and ploughman clearly; photographic reproductions which do not are, for example, in *The Genius of Turner* ed. Holmes, Studio Special Number, 1903; *Gazette des Beaux-Arts* 3. Ser. vol. 32, 1904, facing p. 250; Finberg, op. cit. pl. 22.

57. J. Rewald, *The History of Impressionism* 2nd ed. New York, 1961, p. 258. Even this degree of realism in Monet was not completely satisfactory to some contemporaries: J.-K. Huysmans, in a review of 1880, felt the painter's '*incertaines abréviations*' incapable of rendering '*la colossale ampleur des locomotives et des gares*', which he hoped to see painted in the future. ('L'Exposition des Indépendants en 1880', in *L'Art Moderne*, Paris, 1883 (re-issue Farnborough, 1969) p. 122). John House pointed out this review to me, and also suggested that Monet's earliest known railway painting, *Train dans la Champagne* (Louvre No. 230, repr. H. Bazin, *Impressionist Painting in the Louvre*, London, 1965, p. 291) goes back to before 1870.

58. February 20 1883, C. Pissarro, *Letters to his Son Lucien*, ed. Rewald, 2nd ed. London, n.d. p. 22; also Lucien to Camille, 11 June 1883, in J. Rewald, 'Lucien Pissarro: Letters from London 1883–1891', *Burlington Magazine*, XCI, 1949, p. 189.

59. F. Braquemond, *Du Dessin et de la Couleur*, Paris, 1885, p. 189.

60. P. G. Hamerton, *Turner*, Paris, 1889, p. 94.

61. J. Leclercq, 'J. W. Turner', *Gazette des Beaux-Arts*, op. cit. p. 252.

62. 12 February 1905: L. Venturi, *Les Archives de l'Impressionnisme*, Paris, vol. I, 1939, pp. 400 f.

63. Later in the same volume Turner's *Queen Mab's Grotto* (T.G. 548) was, by some happy coincidence, reproduced, facing p. 253.

64. G. Kahn in *Gazette des Beaux-Arts*, op. cit. pp. 83 f.

65. Lucien Pissarro, loc. cit.; Monet to R. Gimpel in 1918 (R. Gimpel, *Diary of an Art Dealer*, London, 1966, p. 73).

66. Robinson's diary, op. cit. F. Lewison, 'Theodore Robinson and Claude Monet', *Apollo*, LXXVIII, 1963, p. 211. This and the information about Monet's later London visits were kindly supplied by Mr John House.

67. For the sixties, cf. especially W. Bürger, 'J. M. W. Turner', pp. 1, 16, in C. Blanc, T. Gautier, P. A. Jeanron . . . , *Histoire des peintres de toutes les écoles: École Anglaise*, Paris, 1863; E. Chesneau, *L'Art et les Artistes Modernes en France et en Angleterre*, 1864, p. 91; T. Silvestre, 'Documents nouveaux sur E. Delacroix' (1864) in *Les Artistes Français*, I, 1926, pp. 46–7. For the later critics Gage, op. cit. Epilogue.

68. Gage, op. cit. pp. 193 f.

69. *Encyclopédie Française*, XVI, 1935, Ch. II, 3, reprinted in P. Signac, *De Delacroix au neo-impressionnisme*, ed. Cachin, 1964, p. 159.

List of Illustrations

Colour Plate: *Rain, Steam and Speed: The Great Western Railway*. By J. M. W. Turner; exh. 1844. Oil on canvas. London, National Gallery. (Reproduced by courtesy of the Trustees, the National Gallery, London.)

1. *The Railway over Chat Moss*. By T. T. Bury. Lithograph. From *Coloured Views on the Liverpool and Manchester Railway*, 1831. (Reproduced by courtesy of the British Museum.)

2. *Ridley Hall*. By J. W. Carmichael. Engraving. From *Views on the Newcastle and Carlisle Railway*, 1836. (Reproduced by courtesy of the British Museum.)

3. *Snowstorm: Steamboat off a Harbour's Mouth Making Signals in Shallow Water, and going by the Lead. The Author was in this Storm on the Night the Ariel left Harwich*. By J. M. W. Turner; exh. 1842. Oil on canvas. London, Tate Gallery. (Photo: Museum.)

4. *Rain, Steam and Speed*, detail. (Photo: John Webb.)

5. *Rain, Steam and Speed*, detail. (Photo: John Webb.)

6. *Air*. By Benjamin West, *c.* 1780. Oil on canvas. London, Royal Academy of Arts. (Photo: Photo Studios.)

7. *Fire*. By Benjamin West, *c.* 1780. Oil on canvas. London, Royal Academy of Arts. (Photo: Photo Studios.)

8. *Battle Abbey; the Spot where Harold Fell*. Engraved by W. B. Cooke after J. M. W. Turner, 1819. (Photo: Courtauld Institute.)

9a, b. *Apollo and Daphne*. By J. M. W. Turner; exh. 1837. Oil on canvas. London, Tate Gallery. (Photo: Museum.)

10. 'Firefly' Class Locomotive, *Actaeon*, 1841–55. Watercolour. Swindon Public Libraries. (Photo: Dennis H. R. Bird.)

11. *Rain, Steam and Speed*, detail. (Photo: John Webb.)

12. *Maidenhead Railway Bridge*. By J. C. Bourne. Lithograph. From *The History and Description of the Great Western Railway*, London, 1846. (Photo: D. H. R. Bird.)

13. *Cliveden on Thames*. By J. M. W. Turner, *c.* 1807. Oil on canvas. London, Tate Gallery. (Photo: Museum.)

14. *View of the Thames*. By J. M. W. Turner, *c*. 1807. Pencil drawing. London, British Museum, T. B. XCV p. 9. (Photo: Museum.)

15. Frontispiece to Charles Dickens: *Dombey and Son*, 1846. By Phiz (H. K. Browne). (Photo: C. Middleton.)

16. *Rain, Steam and Speed*, detail. (Photo: John Webb.)

17. *An Iron Foundry*. By J. M. W. Turner, *c*. 1797. Watercolour. London, British Museum, T.B. XXXIII B. (Photo: John R. Freeman.)

18. *The Hero of a Hundred Fights*. By J. M. W. Turner, *c*. 1800–1847. Oil on canvas. London, Tate Gallery. (Photo: Museum.)

19. *Oxford from Headington Hill*. By J. M. W. Turner, 1803–4. Watercolour. Oxford, Ashmolean Museum. (Photo: Museum.)

20. *Snowstorm, Mont Cenis*. By J. M. W. Turner, 1820. Watercolour. Birmingham, City Art Gallery. (Photo: City of Birmingham.)

21. *Messieurs les Voyageurs on their return from Italy (Par la Diligence) in a Snowdrift upon Mount Tarrar 22nd of January 1829*. By J. M. W. Turner, exh. 1829. Watercolour. London, British Museum, Lloyd Bequest. (Photo: Museum.)

22. *On the Route through Savoy*. By J. M. W. Turner, 1820. Pencil drawing. London, British Museum, T.B. CXCII p. 18. (Photo: John R. Freeman.)

23. *Staffa: Fingel's Cave*. By J. M. W. Turner, exh. 1832. Oil on canvas. Astor Collection. (Photo: Sydney W. Newbery.)

24. *Rain, Steam and Speed*, detail. (Photo: John Webb.)

25. Detail of 37.

26. *Transept of Ewenny Priory*. By J. M. W. Turner, exh. 1797. Watercolour. Cardiff, National Museum of Wales. (Photo: By permission of the National Museum of Wales.)

27. *Holy Family Resting on the Flight into Egypt*. By Rembrandt van Rijn, 1647. Oil on panel. Dublin, National Gallery of Ireland. (Photo: Courtesy of the National Gallery of Ireland.)

28. *The Unpaid Bill, or the Dentist Reproving his Son's Prodigality*. By J. M. W. Turner, exh. 1808. Oil on panel. Kincaid-Lennox Collection. (Photo: Courtauld Institute of Art.)

29. *The Holy Family*. Attributed to Rembrandt van Rijn. Oil on panel. Amsterdam, Rijksmuseum. (Photo: Museum.)

30. *Rembrandt's Daughter*. By J. M. W. Turner, exh. 1827. Oil on canvas. Cambridge, Mass., Harvard University, Fogg Art Museum. (Photo: Museum.)

31. *Rembrandt's Mistress.* By J. G. Haid, 1767. Mezzotint. Cambridge, Fitzwilliam Museum. (Photo: Museum.)

32. *Joseph accused by Potiphar's Wife.* By Rembrandt van Rijn, 1655. Oil on canvas. Berlin-Dahlem, Staatliche Museum. (Photo: Walter Steinkopf.)

33. *Pilate Washing his Hands.* By J. M. W. Turner, exh. 1830. Oil on canvas. London, Tate Gallery. (Photo: Museum.)

34. *Christ and the Woman taken in Adultery.* By Rembrandt van Rijn, 1644. Oil on panel. London, National Gallery. (Photo: Museum.)

35. *Bonneville, Savoy.* By J. M. W. Turner. 1816. Pen and wash. London, British Museum, T.B. CXVIII J. (Reproduced by courtesy of the British Museum.)

36. *Farm Buildings at the Dijk.* By Rembrandt van Rijn, *c.* 1648. Pen and bistre. London, British Museum, Cracherode Bequest. (Photo: John R. Freeman.)

37. *Landscape with a Coach.* By Rembrandt van Rijn, 1640–41. Oil on panel. London, Wallace Collection. (Photo: Museum.)

38. Detail of 37.

39. *Landscape with a Distant Town.* Attributed to Rembrandt van Rijn. Oil on panel. Lugano, Baron H. Thyssen-Bornemisza Collection.

40. *Grand Junction Canal at Southall Mill.* By J. M. W. Turner, *c.* 1809–10. Oil on canvas. Peter Green Collection.

41. *The Mill.* Attributed to Rembrandt van Rijn. Oil on canvas. Washington, National Gallery of Art. (Photo: Museum.)

42. *Wind, Rain and Sunshine.* By David Cox, 1845. Watercolour. Birmingham, City Art Gallery. (Photo: City of Birmingham.)

43. *The Night Train.* By David Cox, *c.* 1857. Watercolour. Birmingham, City Art Gallery. (Photo: City of Birmingham.)

44. Frontispiece to Pamphlet by G. A. Sala, *c.* 1850. London, British Museum. (Reproduced by courtesy of the British Museum.)

45. *Penge Station, Upper Norwood.* By Camille Pissarro, 1871. Oil on canvas. London, Courtauld Institute Galleries. (Photo: Museum.)

46. *Railway Bridge at Argenteuil.* By Claude Monet, 1875. Oil on canvas. Philadelphia Museum of Art, John G. Johnson Collection. (Photo: Museum.)

47. *Gare St Lazare.* By Claude Monet, 1877. Oil on canvas. Fogg Art Museum, Harvard University, Cambridge, Mass. (Photo: Museum.)

48. *Bristol Station.* By J. C. Bourne. Lithograph. From *The History and*

Description of the Great Western Railway, London, 1846. (Photo: D. H. R. Bird.)

49. *Gare St Lazare.* By Claude Monet, 1877. Oil on canvas. New York, Milliken Collection. (Photo: Helga Photo Studio, Inc.)

50. *Waterloo Bridge – Grey Day.* By Claude Monet, 1903. Oil on canvas. Washington, National Gallery of Art, Chester Dale Collection. (Photo: Museum.)

51. *Die Berlin – Potsdamer Bahn.* By Adolph von Menzel, 1847. Berlin, Nationalgalerie. (Photo: Museum.)

General Reading

Edward Bradbury, 'Picture in Trains', *Magazine of Art*, III, 1880, pp. 107–11.

L. Gowing, *Turner: Imagination and Reality*, New York, 1966.

Graham Reynolds, *Turner*, London, 1969.

J. Kurze, *Die Eisenbahn in der Kunst*, Bild-Jahrbuch der Deutschen Bundesbahn, 1958.

F. D. Klingender, *Art and the Industrial Revolution*, 2nd ed. London, 1968.

Manchester City Gallery, *Art and the Industrial Revolution* (Exhibition catalogue), 1968.

Index

Bold numbers refer to illustration numbers